This Belongs to Us

Stories from UMBC's Founding Four Classes

Collected by Diane Tichnell, Dale Gough, Mimi and Bob Dietrich

UMBC Class of 1970

This Belongs to Us

Stories from UMBC's Founding Four Classes

Collected by Diane Tichnell, Dale Gough, Mimi and Bob Dietrich

UMBC Class of 1970

If these memories from the Founding Four Alumni at

the University of Maryland Baltimore County

inspire you to support UMBC, please consider making a donation to

one of the selected funds of your choice at the UMBC Foundation, Inc. at *umbc.edu/giving/foundingfourbook*.

All contributions are administered by the UMBC Foundation, Inc. for the benefit of UMBC.

ISBN # 9798376700518

Dedication

To the graduates of the Founding Four classes
and all the classes that have followed.

Our Legacy

by Diane Juknelis Tichnell 1970

When I walked on to the UMBC campus for the first time, I felt that something was in the air. It was not just the dust blowing from construction or the weather elements, but something new and fresh.

Fast forward to my mid-life and expressing feelings on this subject to our President Freeman Hrabowski. We needed a book capturing all that was "fresh and new" from those early days. "Write that book!" Dr. Hrabowski replied to me.

When expressing this same feeling to fellow alumni, it became clear to me that we needed to capture the collective memory of those days before, during, and following the birth of the UMBC campus, not just mine...and we needed to capture it now! Not having found the proverbial fountain of youth, I realized that our time is ticking away. We need to tell that story together to properly recreate the mystique of those early years and present it as our legacy. It represents the foundation upon which the current unique UMBC entity rests. If we build it, borrowing from a popular movie, they will come! Potential students can benefit from hearing about the campus roots.

Here are some stories building piece by piece on that founding mystique.

Academic Two Construction, 1971

Introduction

Fields of corn and soy beans. Pigs, a barn and a silo. Summer of 1966 working on the grounds crew. Dr. Kuhn, and Mrs. Kuhn, students, faculty and administrators cleaning and mopping the floor of the cafeteria before opening day. September 19, 1966. Parking in mud. Plywood sidewalks before concrete. Walking to campus from distant bus stops. High school buddies. New classmates who are different. Three buildings. City students. Students from the counties. Microwave cafeteria. Diverse backgrounds. First Generations. Men's sports. Women's sports. The Retriever. Memorable faculty. Inspirational faculty. Civil Rights. Social unrest. Student activism. Hanging out at the cafeteria. Student workers. Studying abroad. The library moves from the 3rd floor of Bldg #1 to the new Library building. "Good morning, UMBC." Hillcrest. Falling in love. Science labs. More buildings rising. Favorite Classes. Invited speakers. Carpooling. "The Concert". Winter Session. A commuter campus gets dorms. Theater productions. The Literary Magazine; and controversy. Protests. Changing majors. Women's issues. Veterans enroll. The Returning Student. Vietnam. More new buildings. "The Red Brick". The Counter Culture. The First (and only) outdoor Graduation (waiting for the rain to stop before chairs could be put in place).

These are just some of the Collective Memories of the first four graduating classes of UMBC, 1970-1973. We have seen its growth from only three buildings to a nationally ranked and internationally known university. We were the beginning, we the "Founding Four".

What follows are the memories of those who chose UMBC when it was an unknown. The stories are in alphabetical order by last name.

Three Original UMBC Buildings 1966

Foreword

The following two pages are
handwritten notes made by Dr. Albin
O. Kuhn, the first Chancellor, as he
travelled the country assembling a
Master Plan for what would become
the University of Maryland, Baltimore
County (UMBC)

What can we do to make campus
life more safer for Day dodgers

1. Parking
2. General Lounge — Hostess - eats (concessions)
   New Lib
3. Improve locker facilities, — general - local
4. Issue lockers on rental basis
   ~~5.~~ — Locker rental on rental to basis
   - Hostess collect rental - not mandatory
5. Decent Lounges — not too formal — Room in a day
   #g the bldgs.
6. Block schedules so that Day dodgers
   have time to use Lib effectively
7. Tying courses together — Block scheduling
8. Improve eating facilities available for
   evening meal.
9. Variety g eating facilities - class 1 2 3 etc
10. more intermural program for day dodger
11. Put in Bowling alleys
12. Research on what student does during
    free time during day
13. Place for clothes for evening events
    showers — toilet facil.
14. Rooms for parents to sit or meet — special
    days — special events

15. Move automats out g many bldgs —
    Students feel part big group.
16. Guest House — Overnight lodging
    for dd.
17. Improve Counceling Center
18. Phils up Static thumbing ride — several
#. marked for where you want to go
19. Set up help to set up car pools
20. Assist in transportation g ss while
    staying out g business
21. Work with public trans interests to
    develop special bus services
22. Develop concept g definate school
    day on campus
23. Get parents help in encouraging a
    full school day
24. Improve coat hangers etc in classrooms
25. Wing Student Union

In His Own Words
Dr. Albin O. Kuhn's handwritten notes as he
traveled on a plane
"at night 2300 over West Virginia".
Note that the first item on his list is "Parking".

"If you bring to the future the same personal qualities and personal commitment you have brought to this campus as students, good and important things will happen to each of you as well as those around you, and the University community will be proud to have played a part in your life."

Dr. Albin O. Kuhn

Chancellor of UMBC 1965-1971

1970 Graduation   June 7, 1970

UMBC First Graduating Class. 1970

Table of Contents - Founding Four Writers

This Belongs to Roslyn Harmon Beaty-Ellis '70, Psychology

A Firm Foundation

I graduated from Edmondson High School in Baltimore, MD in 1966. While attending Edmondson (10th – 12th grade) our school day was reduced to 4-hour shifts due to overcrowding. Having had the importance of education instilled in me at a young age, I chose to attend UMBC for several reasons. It was common knowledge that predominately Caucasian colleges were believed to offer higher quality education, with better access to supporting programs, larger budgets for student needs, more opportunities for growth, and invaluable experiences in the process. Additionally, I saw an opportunity to begin to experience and prepare for life in the real world. One that includes all people, influences, prejudices, differences, and commonalities.

My two older sisters attended and graduated from Morgan State College. My younger sister attended and graduated from Howard University. I completely missed the *"Black College experience"*, but it was my choice. We were raised with the understanding that school wasn't finished until we had a degree. My brother chose to skip college with little repercussions because my parents knew that men had more options and opportunities to make a good living and support a family. On the other hand, they insisted that the girls complete degrees in case they had to take care of themselves and their families. Thank God for insightful parents!

My first day at UMBC was literally a walk through a construction site trying to find my way to the Administration building and then to class. The sidewalks were unfinished and were connected by wooden planks to help you avoid the mud and gravel. There was no landscaping, shelter, or shade apart from the 3 buildings that were certified for occupancy, the Student Union, Lecture Hall, and a Classroom building. The only other building in use was Hillcrest, the Administration building.

The original student body was a class of 750 students, who were excited to be the first to attend UMBC, and the only class ever to have no upperclassmen, as we matriculated from freshman to sophomores, to juniors, and then seniors. We participated in establishing policies and procedures, on-campus groups and clubs, scheduled activities, decided on and named the mascot, and more. The original class, *as I recall* had 13 (or 17?) African American students, including me. Three of us graduated four years later.

Our college years were marked by political dissension and unrest! The unpopular Vietnam War was in full swing, and students were being pulled from school and drafted into the military. Additionally, the Black Power movement was actively defying the status quo, claiming the draft was disproportionately targeting our Black men, and assigning them to units that were first to be called to the front line. Tension was high as the Black Panthers, SNCC and other military-styled groups pulled away from the peaceful protest position and began to arm themselves.

Given the climate in the mid-60s, and the newfound freedom of college life, UMBC was a new experience for me. I was immediately caught up in the thought that at 17, I could choose when I went to class or decided to skip it and play cards in the Student Union. Of course, I chose to learn Double Pinochle. That decision resulted in a 4 credit F in my 1st semester. The good news is that it put me on course to work harder to overcome the effect of that F on my grade point average. I spent the next 3 1/2 years making it up. Aside from my foolish start, I was able to get on track to grow through my experiences at UMBC.

In retrospect, there was clearly segregation on campus at UMBC. It was real but not forced as the students chose to gather, group up, among themselves. Groupings were generally along racial lines and that was our choice. Black power activism was prominent and apparent on every college campus. I wore a large afro and was frequently asked about the Panthers, Black Muslims, and any other Black-related subjects. I remember at some point starting to tell my fellow students that Angela Davis, a well-known Black activist, was my cousin! They believed me!!

The Vietnam War added fuel to the already stressed racial tensions. We lost several of the original Black male pioneers to the draft! Of course, we established a Black Student Union on campus and participated in on-campus demonstrations and protests.

There were opportunities to try to blend socially and the Wednesday Mixers were created for that purpose. This was an attempt to get the students to party together on Wednesday afternoons. I was first introduced to "head-banging" (a type of dancing), at one of these socials. These functions were sparsely attended by Black students. There was, however, a memorable occasion for me, when Otis Redding was presented in concert at a UMBC dance. We had music we enjoyed, a musician who looked like us and we enjoyed his special attention since we were so few! It was a special night!

My memories of classroom experiences at UMBC include my 4 credit, 8:00 AM Calculus class in the Lecture Hall. The class time was early, the subject matter was boring and the professor struggled to engage the students. Staying awake in class was the main objective. On another note, I remember my Sociology classes with Dr. Rothstein. Often the only Black student in class, if not one of two, I sat as he taught about the obstacles associated with growing up Black in the inner city. It was an uncomfortable experience, exaggerated by the social issues of the times. My first-hand experience could not and was not adequately conveyed through theories of what it means to grow up Black. When asked directly, I felt that in my attempts to add clarification, I was seen as a specimen under a microscope. As a result, I made little effort to expose myself to their judgment.

Because many of my pioneer Black classmates were being drafted or otherwise dropping out of school, the pool of close associates continued to narrow. There were two ladies Beverly Rankin, and Gail Williams with whom I became friends. Gail, Beverly, and I were the last of the Black pioneers and we provided each other with mutual support, companionship, understanding, and encouragement. We completed our bachelor's degree programs at UMBC, fully aware of the magnitude of the feat. We've gone our separate ways but I pray that all is well with my friends.

As I look back on my four years at UMBC, it really feels as though I was an observer rather than a participant, learning not only the subject matter but the ways of those who were different from me. Clearly, at that time, there was no "real" place for those of us who took this venture. Apparently, I did achieve my goals, being immersed in a mini white world to prepare me for the plunge into the real world. I observed, I studied, I learned in the classroom and I grew. The value of a good education has always been seen as an equalizer, (or at least a step in the right direction), for people who are prejudged or otherwise categorized.

After graduation, I spent 6 years working as a Caseworker at the Maryland Reception Diagnostic and Classification Center, located in the Maryland Penitentiary. I did some graduate work at the University of Baltimore before relocating to Houston, TX. I worked at the Harris County Juvenile Probation Department, in Houston for more than 30 years, before retiring from the position of Deputy Director of Human Resources in 2011. My three children, Stacey Allen a full-time mom, having raised 7 children, my son Dr. Claude A. Beaty, Jr., a Pediatric Cardio-Thoracic Surgeon and father of 4, and my youngest, Lindsey Beaty, Esq. an attorney and mother of two, keep me busy when I'm not working with the church, traveling or trying to stay fit.

Ultimately, real growth lies in the realization of God's word and His saving grace. I am so grateful for His hand on my life and my family! I thank God that though the road to eliminate racial bias has been long, slow and hard, society as a whole is making progress towards erasing racial boundaries. I pray that all current UMBC students and graduates are fully immersed in their education and thoroughly enjoying the experience! I am happy to have been a part of establishing a firm foundation for those who followed!

1970 Graduates

This Belongs to Jay Berg '70, Biological Sciences

Three Buildings and Mud

Three buildings and mud. That is the answer I always give when someone asks me what I recall about my first year at UMBC in 1966. Wiping my soiled shoes as I walked into Lecture Hall 1 on September 19, 1966, I began my journey into adulthood as a biology major. It seemed most of the students in my class majored in biology as pre-med. Me? Well I never knew what I wanted to be when I grew up and, since I was always interested in science, I thought this was the most obvious route to take.

After spending three years at an all-male high school (Baltimore City College), it was pretty interesting being among females in an academic setting for the first time since junior high. Unfortunately, there weren't a great amount of ladies to flirt with. In fact, to my chagrin, it seemed that there were many more males than females. And most of them seemed more interested in the best looking professor on campus (American Studies Prof Joel Jones).

My freshman beginning was harrowing. Because the folks in the Registrar Office neglected to send my name to the local draft board certifying my student status, I received that dreaded greetings letter from the U.S. Army instructing me to report for my induction a couple of weeks before my first class. The good news was that I could appeal, and likely win, with submission of the proper certification. The bad news was that decision wouldn't be in time for the induction - so I actually had to go through the entire grueling process that took all day beginning at 5:30am in Reisterstown, Maryland. I don't have to tell you the utter fear I had listening to my position in the first draft lottery in late 1968 after already experiencing that dreaded "You're In the Army Now" process. My whole life literally flashed before my eyes as I huddled around a radio while ping pong balls were utilized to first pick the draft order number followed by a bouncing ball with a birth date. At the conclusion, luckily, my date scored a 262 immediately surrounded by very low numbers. However, I still sweated it out. The Army needed a huge initial recruitment and reached #200 in the initial two weeks. They stopped recruiting at #224. (As it turns out, the draft did not go above number 25 any year thereafter.) Losing a couple of years off of my life during that ordeal, I went on to complete four years, while witnessing the campus expand to such an extent that, by graduation day, it was barely recognizable from the three-buildings-and-mud memory impaled in my brain forever. I distinctly remember sitting on the open UMBC field outside the Faculty Office Building, along with 250 of the original 750 freshman on a glorious graduation day on June 7, 1970. As I listened to a commencement speech given by the late veteran ABC News reporter and co-anchor, Howard K. Smith, I experienced a solid sense of accomplishment and pride of being a member of the first class to receive a UMBC diploma. At the same time, a certain sense of dread hovered over me as I realized that I still didn't know what I was going to do when I grew up.

A couple of my most notable and vivid recollections during those 4 years:

– I always enjoyed writing. So when the call went out for contributors to our newly formed campus newspaper, I volunteered. I started as a features reporter and later became the Features Editor. (I've since carried that passion forward. As a movie buff, I became an online review/commentary blogger in 2008 and write occasionally as a freelance writer covering film festivals for an online film site. If you're interested in my writings, search my name.)

– Music has also always been a part of my life. I was the concert master in my Junior High orchestra and have seen hundreds of concerts from classical to rock during my lifetime. When Otis Redding and his 12-piece orchestra played on April 22, 1967 in the gymnasium (with the worst acoustics imaginable), I was in the first row pressed against the stage. (I believe I can still feel his sweat spraying on me during his two-set performance.) Tragically, Otis died in a plane crash less than 5 months later on December 10th. On October 19, 1969 a seven-member jazz rock orchestra named Chicago Transit Authority played two shows right after their brilliant debut album was released. They eventually changed their name to Chicago and have since produced over 40 albums (five #1) and sixty-four singles (21 made the top-10). It was around this time that I was living out another dream. From 1967-1971 I was a lead singer in several rock bands, one of which actually played at UMBC in 1971.

– From April 6 to April 14, 1968 civil unrest hit Baltimore, one of 100 cities that reacted to the assassination of Martin Luther King on April 4. Crowds filled the streets, local businesses were burned and looted while police and the National Guard were confronted by the mob. My Editor, Diane Juknelis, reminded me of her fear when I told her in April 1968 that I was heading to my parent's pizza shop in Brooklyn Park south of Baltimore City to defend against any possible damage. Luckily, none of the rioters went south of Baltimore, so I am happily still here to report on it.

– In 1969 the Vietnam War was raging. The Red Brick, a campus political activist newspaper was created accompanied by much controversy. In April, a major protest occurred on campus over promotion and tenure issues in which a large number of students, including myself, occupied the hallways of Hillcrest, the administration building, for three days and three nights. Student dissension for all kinds of reasons across the country reached a crescendo in 1970 – especially after the Kent State massacre on May 4th. Locally, a peace march was organized to walk down Frederick Road in Catonsville in front of an induction center. Stirring contention here on campus, Yippie leader Abbie Hoffman was invited and spoke as part of a "political/rock program" along with counterculture figures journalist/comedian Paul Krassner and musicians David Peel and The Lower East Side. The peaceful serenity I experienced September 19, 1966 seemed a hundred years off.

Upon graduating, after being enthralled with the romanticism of several Jacques Cousteau specials I saw on TV, I had the somewhat unrealistic vision of being an oceanographer. I actually secured an interview with Boston University for their marine biology graduate program. However, I ultimately passed on that dream when I found out that my career path would (UGH!) involve teaching, which I had absolutely no interest in, and not classical adventures sailing on the open seas. I had a short-lived thought of becoming a radio DJ after rooming with a progressive radio host from the Baltimore progressive AM station WAYE. That was followed by stints as a biology lab assistant with NIH and Johns Hopkins, with a very brief stop in dental school (I didn't really want to put my hands in peoples' mouths for the rest of my life) sandwiched in-between. After my dreams of becoming a rock star faded into stark reality, I finally came to my senses, settled down (somewhat) and spent nearly 38 years working for SSA. I thankfully retired in 2012.

Serendipity entered my life while living blocks from The Charles Theater for 30 years, which brought me in contact with Pat Moran. She managed the single screen (at the time) movie palace and our friendship brought me in direct contact with filmmaker John Waters. Pat was John's life-long casting agent. She later opened her own casting agency in Baltimore and has since won three casting Emmys for productions filmed in and around Baltimore. I became a non-speaking extra in several productions including "Major League II", Barry Levinson's "Avalon" (where I worked all day with a 9-year-old Elijah Wood) and a couple of episodes of "Homicide-Life on the Streets". One of these episodes was starring the late Robin Williams who was nominated for an acting Emmy. The episode won a Writers Guild of America Award for Best Screenplay of an Episodic Drama. Eating lunch on the courthouse steps with the late great comedian will be a special lifelong memory. And, while working as an IT Specialist at SSA, my co-worker for several years who worked 15 feet across the aisle was none other than David Gluck. David had an extremely memorable part in Waters' cult classic "Pink Flamingos". For anyone who has seen the film, David was the performer at Divine's birthday party. No further explanation will be made here for obvious reasons. Suffice it to say, John Waters specifically mentioned David's "talent" while touting the 25th anniversary of "Pink Flamingos" on Johnny Carson's

Tonight Show back in the 90s. The otherwise quiet, reserved Mr. Gluck was beaming with pride the next day!

Besides movies and music, my other passion is sports. On March 16, 2018 when the Retrievers beat #1 Virginia in the March Madness Basketball tournament, tears literally flowed down my face. UMBC, after 48 years was finally on the map, and not as some religious institution as some in the media had initially proclaimed.

When people ask me what I'm currently doing, I always answer, "Anything I freakin' want." That being said, I still really don't know what I want to be when I grow up.

After UMBC:

- Worked briefly at NIH and Johns Hopkins University as a lab technician
- Worked from 1974-2012 for the Social Security Administration until retiring as an IT Specialist
- Worked from 1989-2001 as a part time pari-mutuel teller at Maryland race tracks; and from 2001-on, worked at race tracks around the country for major thoroughbred races, including the Triple Crown and Breeders Cup
- From 2008-2020, maintained a movie review and commentary blog ("Jay Berg's Cinema Diary") and served as a freelance contributor to the online international movie site Film Festival Today

Otis Redding at UMBC, 1967

This Belongs to Rebecca Leisure Berkeley '70, Biological Sciences

Taking That Next Step at UMBC

I walked onto the UMBC campus excited! There was so much potential here and I felt I had the opportunity to learn so many new things. In addition, it seemed that this was going to be a lot of fun too! I wanted a broad educational experience and this was the place to get it!

Looking back on the campus then, I saw it as an intriguing place physically, an awesome place educationally, and a fun place socially. Everything was brand new and the door was wide open to prepare myself in a comprehensive way for a career in the library field. I was ready to soak up all knowledge and experiences like a sponge! Let's go!

My first impressions of the campus were filled with curiosity about the land upon which it was built. There was the "swamp", a lake-like body of water between the classroom buildings and the partially finished library. Passing through that area in a day or pausing between classes, made us truly "lunch" for the bugs! I recall the trips to and from the campus as a series of rides, paying for gas, and parking all over the place on this commuter campus. All of these experiences were good intermediate steps to find yourself after high school. It gave you parameters and made you ready for life. It opened your eyes. For instance, I found that smoking made me cough!

As a History major with a minor in English, I found myself drawn to the Film Club viewing mainly foreign films which were cheap, and to the Literary Magazine which had a colorful and often controversial impact on the campus. We had great faculty, especially in the language areas of Latin, French, German, and Spanish. My eyes continued to be opened by Dr. Augustus Low and the Black Studies courses. The fact that these courses were not taught anywhere else at that time made the experience of them even more significant.

Then there are the fun memories of sneaking pizza into the study carrels and shooting each other with "toothpick tubes" or straws converted into toothpick projectile launchers. I had the honor of placing in a pizza eating contest where the mantra was "eat as though there is no tomorrow!"

The highlight of the time at UMBC had to be the MiniMester or winter session as it is now termed. A trip featuring Latin Classical Studies took us on a memorable journey to Great Britain, conjuring up thoughts of "shillings in the meter" at Victoria Station and attending a performance of the musical Hair in London.

Traveling to Rome on a train in hot weather and the swing through the treasures of the Vatican unprotected in many cases, remain special memories today.

However, not all the time in Europe was spent in disco clubs peering through smoke to view lighted disco floors. There was studying to do and quizzes to take along the way. Amidst the small quarters in Paris, the many baguettes, and the small bottles filled with green liquor, the instructors stayed in step with us and immersed us in the various cultures, meeting friendly people along the way.

Through my career years at the Enoch Pratt Free Library, and while pursuing my MS in Information Science at Drexel, and my MBA in Business Administration at the University of Baltimore, my UMBC experiences instilled a desire to keep faithful to both traveling and learning.

After UMBC:

- Obtained a scholarship to go to Drexel - MLS degree
- Received MBA from University of Baltimore
- Worked at Enoch Pratt Free Library
- Got married - two children
- Son Lewis Berkeley - graduated from UMBC
- Continued traveling (inspired by the MiniMester at UMBC)
- Traveled to: China, Japan, Singapore, Australia, New Zealand, Russia, England, Sweden, Norway, Brazil, India, Nepal, Egypt, Greece, Italy, Spain, France, Thailand, Argentina, Chile, Peru (climbed Machu Picchu) plus traveled in the United States.
- "I plan to continue traveling in the future."

This Belongs to Ed Berlin '70, History

Finding the Larger Perspective

After my first year, just about everyone I knew from high school transferred to College Park. The small Jewish group I hung out with in between classes was about to get smaller. Much smaller.

Guys I knew from high school, and some as far back as elementary school, were leaving. And my routine of playing cards with my old pals in the Student Union was about to vanish.

Even Susan Wagner, one of the few new friends I had made at UMBC, was planning to transfer to Mary Washington College at the University of Virginia. Susan and I had met in the book line one rainy morning, and we had become fast friends.

I worried that this was going to be a very lonely year.

There were lots of reasons why people were leaving. Some wanted to take courses that were not being offered as part of the school's small but expanding curriculum. Others had always planned to go away to school but their families felt they needed one more year at home. Still others felt a UMBC education was second rate. UMBC, apparently, did not match their personal self-image. This perspective obviously turned out to be shortsighted.

Then there was the social aspect. No fraternities or sororities. Not enough campus entertainment and social experiences.

And, of course, there was the issue of culture. In the case of some of my Jewish friends from high school, there was a sense of alienation from a predominantly Christian culture. Baltimore was, and still is, a mosaic of neighborhoods, separating social and religious tribes that rarely came into contact, if at all. Oriole and Colt games, jury duty, etc. Many people still believed in sticking with their own kind.

Nonetheless, I entered my sophomore year with a sense of anticipation rather than dread. UMBC was still new to me. New buildings, new teachers. And, as it turned out, new friends. Friends from Arbutus, Dundalk, Towson, Edmondson Village, Hampden. Neighborhoods I rarely if ever visited. From schools I had not heard of: Archbishop Curley, Cardinal Gibbons, Mount St. Agnes, Calvert Hall.

I met a bunch of new people: John Rosche, Carrol Clarke, Chris Monahan, Betty Titsworth, Kenny Knapp, Larry Blotzer, Peter Caruso, John King. Getting to know each of them opened up my world.

The school was small. I guess it was easier to meet people since there were so few of us. And we were all in the same boat, each trying to find our way. We were pioneers. Despite our different backgrounds, we realized how much we had in common. It was great. Meeting people from different places turned out to be just as valuable to me as the coursework.

Peter and John remain friends of mine to this day.

My high school, City College, was fully integrated. It was an urban school. An ethnic school. About everyone I knew there was Black, or of Jewish or Greek descent. And it was an all-boys school.

UMBC introduced me to the broader America – predominantly white, Christian. It would be the America in which I would work, build a career, and raise a family. I realized there was room for me, and I decided that I wanted to make room in my life for all types of people. I still had a bunch of Jewish friends at school – Dan Shub, Joel Lowenstein, among others. But they were part of a larger, diverse community.

Some people call this assimilation. I call it the American family. Like all families, it was far from perfect. But it worked.

Today, the American family continues to be a work in progress. Many people continue to be short changed. As we speak, this sense of family is at risk. Some people have pulled back, preferring to stay within their familial tribe. Suspicious of other people's intentions or placing their own culture above others. Not believing that there is room in America for all of us.

Those of us that attended UMBC know better. We cannot allow this. Like our alma mater, our country was built through contributions by Black, Asian, Latin, and European peoples. Jewish, Christian, believers, and non-believers alike. Through shared effort and tolerance.

This is the UMBC legacy I value the most.

After UMBC:

- Received a Master's Degree in International Relations from NYU
- Started career as an attorney at the Federal Communications Commission and Citibank in New York.
- Became a designer of electronic services at Deutche Bank and Thomson-Reuters, managed trading floor technology for Citibank
- Owned an independent bookshop in Baltimore, wrote a book, and published an arts magazine, BmoreArt.
- Married to Ann Garlington Berlin for 43 years.
- Two children, Sam, living in Plymouth England, and Maria, who lives in Baltimore. She is the mother of our two grandchildren, Isobel and Michaela.
- "UMBC was my Launchpad."

This Belongs to Gabija Brazauskas Blotzer '70, English

The First Student

Acquiring the distinction of being "UMBC's First Student to Register" was not an honor that I had sought intentionally. Originally, I did not intend to go to UMBC because I had applied and had been accepted to the University of Maryland College Park campus. However since my housing application was misplaced and had no dormitory room assignment, I decided to enroll at UMBC. Regrettably I have no vivid memories of what transpired during my morning course selection meeting at the Registrar's office other than that there was no special fanfare.

Returning to UMBC as a "special" student twice over a span of 18 years to take additional courses proved to be a more valuable experience for me than being the first student to register. After attending Duke University Graduate School, I first registered at UMBC as a "special" student during the summer term of 1971 to fulfill several mandatory education courses in order to obtain a Professional Certificate to teach English in the state of Maryland. Then years later during the fall term of 1989, I returned a second time as a "special" student to acquire a second certification to teach Latin in Pennsylvania. I owe a great debt to the late Professor Walter Sherwin who accepted me back in 1989 as a very rusty Latin student and offered me the support needed to once again translate ancient Latin texts. Throughout my years at UMBC, Walter Sherwin was a valuable mentor to me.

As an undergraduate at UMBC I received a solid education in the liberal arts, and as a "special" returning student I achieved a lifetime career as a teacher.

Latin Lovers

My initial introduction to Professor Walter Sherwin occurred during the fall semester of 1966 when I took his English 111, World Literature in translation, class. One day outside of the classroom, he and I casually spoke about our mutual interest in classical literature, and he mentioned that he was a Latin instructor. When I shared with him that I had taken 4 years of Latin at Western High School, Professor Sherwin convinced me to take his Classics 301, Advanced Latin Readings translation class during the following spring semester. Upon reporting to the first day of class, I realized that the assigned room was Professor Sherwin's office. Haltingly I walked in, saw another student, a young man, already sitting inside, and realized that this was both the location and the total enrollment for the class. As I processed the scene before me, a refrain from a 1965 hit song flashed through my mind, "Nowhere to run to, baby. Nowhere to hide." At that time and for several years afterwards, I did not appreciate the fact that as a freshman I was given the extraordinary opportunity to take a 300 level course, receiving Dr. Sherwin's undivided attention and obtaining practically one on one instruction. Over my years as a student at UMBC, I took 8 various classes taught by Dr. Sherwin and found him to be a man of wisdom and compassion, who was never overbearing. He took a genuine interest in his students and instilled in them an appreciation and love of the classics. He always found time to speak with me about academic and personal issues, even when I became an English, and not a Latin, major. It was my honor to have known Dr. Sherwin over the years. He was responsible for molding me into the Latin teacher that I became.

After UMBC:

- Received MA in English from Duke University
- Taught high school English in Howard County, MD and high school Latin in York, PA from 1972 to 2014
- Visited relatives in Lithuania in 1975, 1980, 1985, and 2015
- Volunteers for one of the York County PA Libraries

Dr. Walter Sherwin, Classics

This Belongs to Lawrence M. Blotzer '70, Economics

OK Dad, It's a Deal

I graduated from high school in '66 and had no interest in going to college. There were better things to do than sit in a classroom, like ride a motorcycle. My father thought otherwise (I think the draft and Vietnam War influenced his thinking) and offered to buy me a sports car if I went to UMBC. Okay dad, it's a deal. When I went to register my advisor loaded me up with courses I had little interest in (at least that's my excuse) and I was placed on academic probation after the first semester. My father said okay, if you want to join the Marines, go ahead. But I viewed it as a challenge, wanted to prove that I could be successful in college.

Next semester I took a Statistics course with Professor Robinson. Brilliant man and a chain smoker who taught with a cigarette in one hand and chalk in the other. One day after class I asked him how much he studied when he was a student at Johns Hopkins and he said that every evening he would sit in an easy chair and read for a couple hours. Oh to be so smart.

Racism was alive and well in 1966. I took an American History class and the professor taught that the Civil War was not fought because of slavery. Guess she got her PhD down South.

After UMBC:

- Worked for Department of Defense 1971-2009
- Daughter born in 1982, son in 1985
- Divorced in 2005
- Lives in Battle Ground, WA
- Still enjoys riding a motorcycle!

Easy Riders

This Belongs to Bob Bolton '70, Mathematics and Elinora Bolton '70, French

An Interrupted Education Completed

In the late 1960s, Bob Bolton '70, mathematics, caught glimpses of his mother around UMBC's new relatively small campus. While he was heading to or from class, he'd spot her in the French Department, where Elinora Bolton '70, French, was getting her undergraduate degree, or in the library, studying.

"It was quieter than at home," Bolton says, laughing. He had nine brothers and sisters, and most of them still lived in their Elkridge home at the time.

In spring of 1970, Bob in his cap and gown followed his 52-year-old mother, in her own commencement regalia, across the stage. Mother and son were awarded their undergraduate degrees in the same first graduating class of UMBC.

"I was so proud of her," said Bolton, the second son in the family and now the chief executive officer of an actuarial firm. "I didn't really appreciate then how hard it was for her."

A tribute to the matriarch

In 2018, Bolton wanted to honor his mother, and all his family. So he endowed the Bolton Family Scholarship, to support two students annually in UMBC's Individualized Studies Program (INDS), with stipends of $1,000 a semester. "Education was the most important thing" to his parents, Bolton says, though they were agnostic about their fields of study. "They gave us no particular direction, they just made sure we were well educated."

Bolton explains that he chose to give the scholarship to INDS majors to reflect the breadth of interests of the Bolton family members who attended UMBC, studying everything from math and music to French, sociology, and geography.

"The INDS program is grateful for the generosity of the Bolton family," says Carrie Sauter '96, psychology, INDS assistant director. "Their commitment to support the INDS student community offers a wonderful family tribute of hard work and success."

An international childhood

Born into Baltimore society in the elegant townhouse that is now the Brewer's Art restaurant, Elinora Bowdoin moved to France at age 7 with her mother and sister after her parents' divorce, according to Steve Bolton, her son and family historian. At 18, Elinora was presented in a flowing white dress to King George VI, Steve says. She studied at the Sorbonne in Paris for 18 months, but the onset of World War II and her mother's death interrupted her education.

Elinora and her sister returned to Baltimore in 1939. "Feeling foreign" and a bit at sea, Steve says. The sisters kept themselves busy with becoming nationally ranked as tennis doubles champions, and attending balls at elegant locations, such as the Alcazar Hotel (now the Baltimore School for the Arts), where Elinora met her future husband in 1940.

Robert Harrison Bolton was a pilot in the Army Air Corps and married Elinora on a three-day pass. Their first child was born in 1944, and for more than 20 years, Elinora stayed home to raise her children. The family remembers her as an energetic mother, an indifferent cook, and an avid reader.

"She did have the life of the mind," Steve says.

A family tradition

The same year her tenth and final child entered kindergarten, Elinora started at UMBC. Her records from the Sorbonne were lost in the war, so she began again at the beginning. Almost tripped up by having to kill and dissect a frog in a biology course, Elinora persevered for four years while her "well-trained" children looked after one another when she was on campus, Bob says.

After her graduation from UMBC, she remained close friends with May Roswell, a UMBC founder who established the modern languages department. Elinora went on to earn her master's degree in French literature at the University of Maryland, College Park, and teach for decades at UMBC, College Park, and Catholic University. She died in 2012 at the age of 92.

Following mother and son's trailblazing graduation, the family has established a legacy at UMBC. In 1975, Chris, another of Elinora's sons graduated with a degree in sociology, and in 1986 her two youngest, Andy and Jim, graduated together with degrees in music and sociology, respectively. Her granddaughter Erin Bolton, geography, graduated from UMBC in 1999.

Education is a family tradition. At their childhood home, complete with a family goat and all those siblings, the brothers remember their mother's books and papers spread out on the dining room table, evidence of her life of the mind. But mostly Elinora studied outside her house. It was quieter.

After UMBC:

- Founder and Chairman of Bolton USA, an employee benefits, actuarial, investment and compensation consulting firm.
- Fellow of the Society of Actuaries and Fellow of the Conference of Consulting Actuaries.
- Partner with brother Andrew, also a UMBC grad, in rehabilitating historic properties.
- Active on community and school boards.
- Coached rec baseball and AAU basketball.
- Married Linda Gaibers in 1968. Two sons, Chad in 1970 and Chris in 1975
- Linda died in 1984. Married Diana DePasquale in 1992, divorced in 2009. Married Eve Mędrek in 2014.
- Lives in Highland Beach, Florida and Rehoboth Beach, Delaware

Note: This story was included with the permission of Jenny O'Grady, editor, UMBC Magazine, May 2021, written by Susan Thornton Hobby

Procession of First Graduates, June 7, 1970

This Belongs to Richard Bond '70, Psychology

Lacrosse and Flying

By my senior year at UMBC there were three of us who were on the lacrosse team who were also doing volunteer work for a local youth organization: myself, Tom Pilsch, who was a starting midfielder, and Neil Duddy, who was our starting goalie. Both of these guys were not only teammates; they also were very close friends. Tom was to be in my wedding and to this day, remains a close friend.

Every now and then our involvement in lacrosse conflicted with our commitment to our volunteer work, one of which was a spring conference that year that took place right in the middle of lacrosse season. As a senior I was a candidate to become the first All American athlete in the (short) history of UMBC. So, missing a game, for me, was not an option. At the same time, for three starters to miss a game would place our team in a real bind. What to do? I had an idea.

The conference was a few hours' drive to the east, in Atlantic City, New Jersey. The game, scheduled on the Saturday of the weekend conference, was against Western Maryland College, and located a few hours' drive west of UMBC. There was obviously no way we could drive to the game from the conference, and back. However, we were not to be deterred. We knew that the conference schedule had a big chunk of free time in the middle of Saturday afternoon, which was when the game was scheduled to be played. We figured if we flew instead of driving, we could get to the game, play, and get back by dinnertime to the conference. I'm not talking about commercial flying, as the only airport near where the game was being played was a private strip that had a grass runway. "Roads? Where we're going, we don't need roads."

Terry was a friend who lived down the block from me, and even though he was only 18, he already had his pilot's license. Imagine this idea coming to life in my head, then convincing this student to fly me and two other lacrosse players from Atlantic City to western Maryland, and back. Then I had to sell the idea to Tom and Neil. Finally, I had to convince our coach to let us fly in for the game. But that's exactly what we did. Teleportation wouldn't be invented for a few hundred years. (Even then, it didn't end well for the Fly.)

Terry had gotten his pilot's license less than a year before. His lessons were taken while flying a Piper Cherokee, which is a low wing plane, that is, the wing is located below the fuselage as opposed to above it. But because we were departing from Atlantic City, we had to rent a plane that was available there. And the only four place single engine plane available was a Cessna 172, which is a high wing plane-not a plane that Terry was certified to fly. No problem. Tom, Neil, and I, along with Terry, had arrived in Atlantic City Friday night when the conference began. We drove Terry to the airport in Atlantic City early Saturday morning.

In order to get certified to fly the Cessna, Terry had to go up with an instructor and pass a flight test. And if he didn't pass, the whole plan would be a bust for us in terms of ever getting to our lacrosse game. Fortunately, Terry passed.

By lunchtime Terry and the three of us were at the airport and took off for western Maryland and the lacrosse game. My parents planned to meet us at the little airport at our destination with all of our equipment so we didn't have to take it on the plane. We arrived with just enough time to land and get a ride to the game. However, we encountered a slight problem. We couldn't find the tiny airport! There was no "tower" per se, but just a small office at the strip. A grass landing field in the midst of rolling hills and pastureland isn't exactly the easiest thing to see. Several times we thought we saw it, only to get close and realize it wasn't the airport. Terry started to get frustrated, and smooth flying slowly deteriorated into, "Darn, that's not it," a sharp yank on the controls and a steep turn to get over the next hill and look more. By the time we finally found the runway, not only were we late, everyone except Terry was about to lose their lunch from the up, down and twisty flying.

My parents were relieved to have us finally arrive and whisked us off to Western Maryland College and the game. But because we were late by then, we only arrived as the team was heading out to the field for warm up. No problem. We rushed and got our equipment on and ran out well before the game started. Yes, a problem. Our coach, whose tolerance was already stretched to the limit in the first place, had become further irritated by our tardiness and decided to impose a penalty. All three of us had to sit on the bench for the entire first quarter. Not only did this give our team a distinct disadvantage, with three of the ten starters out, it also didn't exactly ingratiate us to our teammates.

I don't recall the score that day, but I know that we won the game. I scored a fair number of goals, and every one of them was an "angry" goal. I was angry that we had to sit on the bench for the first quarter, and yet had gone through so much trouble, not to mention personal expense, to get to the game. So, I was going to take it out on the other team. By the end of the game all was forgiven by both our teammates and the coach. Winning can do that for you. Had we lost it may have been a different story altogether.

The Return Trip

We didn't have much time to get back to Atlantic City, so my folks drove us right back to the little airport. We all jumped into the plane and in short order Terry had us rolling down the runway for takeoff. Except that we began to encounter one slight difficulty; we weren't taking off! About half way down the runway Terry and I exchanged concerned glances, and at about the same time we realized the problem. The Piper plane, with which Terry was familiar, required a certain degree of flaps for takeoff. So, when we started down the runway that day, Terry lowered the flaps. But what the instructor failed to communicate earlier was that a Cessna's takeoff with the degree of flaps we were using would inhibit the forward speed of the plane. On top of that, we were on a grass runway, and one where there had been a lot of spring rainfall which made taking off more sluggish and slow. We were rapidly running out of runway!

My parents, who were witnessing this entire take off, and having no idea what was going on in the cockpit, had a real moment of panic. My Dad had suffered a heart attack the year before. When I finally got back home after the conference and we were talking about that takeoff, my Mom told me that Dad had to take one of his nitroglycerin pills.

Finally, we were in the air and headed back to our conference. All day we had enjoyed beautiful weather. But wouldn't you know it, the closer we got to Atlantic City, storm clouds began to close in and the visibility dropped. When small, piston engine planes with carburetors descend rapidly, especially in changing and cooling weather, condensation can form inside the carburetor that can actually wind up freezing, which then causes the engine to stop running. Not good. As we crossed the end of the runway, the engine conked out completely. Terry and I exchanged a glance that looked like the two guys in the crow's nest on the Titanic when they first saw the iceberg. We were looking at the propeller. Shouldn't that thing have been turning round and round? Instead, it was just sitting there smiling at us.

Fortunately, we did have enough momentum that Terry executed a perfect "dead stick" landing. In spite of multiple, potentially fatal errors, Tom and Neil, in the backseat were, for the large part, blissfully ignorant. Terry and I on the other hand, could have used one of my Dad's pills. It made for fun story telling when we got back to school, but I'll always remember it as one of the most fun/scary events of my UMBC college experiences.

After UMBC:

- Received Masters in Theology, Fuller Theological Seminary.
- Professionally worked for a non-profit youth organization for 20 years after graduating, and later worked for an international missions based non-profit, directing

the Life Coaching program for approximately 2,000 mostly indigenous leadership, worldwide. This job involved extensive overseas traveling, especially to Africa, Eastern and Western Europe, Asia, and the Pacific, visiting over 50 nations during that time.

- Continued playing lacrosse in the USCLA (United States Club Lacrosse Association) for eight years (no pro field lacrosse back then), winning four national championships.
- Coached high school lacrosse for eight years, twice Florida Coach of the Year and won a Florida State Championship.
- Married to Carol Hesson Bond, also class of 1970, for 51 years.
- "Lacrosse was such a big part of my UMBC memories."

UMBC Lacrosse Team, 1969

This Belongs to Barbara Callan Bradshaw '73, Psychology

UMBC and Women's Sports - the EARLY years

In 1968, going to UMBC meant two things to me; determining a major that would get me a job and playing women's basketball a little longer. There were no dreams of scholarships, shoe contracts, fame, or fortune. This was 1968-1972, that was the stuff of daydreams. Title IX was enacted weeks AFTER I graduated. And UMBC Intercollegiate athletics was in its infancy as a new school. There were no long held rivalries or past defeats to overcome. And, honestly, the infrastructure was in its infancy, too.

There was one gymnasium (The "Multi-Purpose Building", as all buildings were appropriately named in the early days). The men's athletic programs garnered all the prime practice/use time. The school's Physical Education teachers doubled as coaches. Both men's and women's teams got uniforms, usually black and gold with UMBC emblazoned on them. The difference then was that the women had the same uniform of all three sports in my first year: Field Hockey, Basketball and Volleyball. It was a black gabardine jumper with a sash and bloomers. It was supposed to be worn with a white blouse with "peter-pan" collar, which we were instructed to buy at the bookstore. This was the same blouse that women taking Phys Ed had to wear in gym class and purchase at the bookstore. Women had to launder their own uniforms and supply their own shoes in the early years. There were no team managers and supplies were limited for women's teams, too. I remember one away-game where we only had one ice pack for school injuries and three athletes with bad ankles and knees. The school did supply buses for away games but it was slow to fund any overnight stays for the women's games. That finally happened when we played Frostburg State College and Salisbury State in '70 or '71. Toward the end of my tenure, the Equipment room changed to offer both men and women athletes a "full" issue (shirt, shorts, socks, towel). Prior to that, women were only given a towel.

This seems like a tale of woe but it is part of the early history at UMBC and how things were 50 years ago. It also gives a perspective to the tremendous changes and improvements that UMBC has embraced by the political and cultural changes I have experienced in these past 50+ years. In fact, other than that hot, heavy uniform, my UMBC sports memories are filled with the fun, the camaraderie, and the awe of the achievements we made with our grit, skill, and determination for our little unknown school. Those hard-fought battles on the various courts of play forged lifelong friendships that still endure. And I remember the dedicated, caring coaches who were equally as ecstatic as we were when we won and as pained when we lost. We sang old time songs and folk songs on the bus rides, we celebrated equally our victories and our defeats, often at Father's Ice Cream Parlor in Catonsville and enjoyed our team spirit.

I had a very traditional and disciplined first 12 years of schooling, consisting of all catholic education / influence. I lived close by to UMBC. I think I only applied to UMBC, which is most unlike today's high school seniors 5, 6, 7 or more applications.

I started my first day at college (class of 1973) having purchased all of the textbooks for the first semester classes. And you guessed it, I carried all of the textbooks for that first day. I think they were wrapped with that very effective rubber strap with a hook closure. When my sister saw me (she was a year ahead of me), she tried to muffle that laugh that would eventually release into a derision.

I also entered my first lecture hall class, which I found exhilarating and somehow important that I was there. But later, I discovered that the smaller classes zeroed in on the subject. You got to know the professor and the other students. There were more conversations and opinions allowed.

After UMBC:

- Worked for the Federal government as a program analyst
- Married with 3 children and 7 grandchildren
- "I am most proud of my children who have obtained Bachelors' degrees and Masters' degrees and are very successful in their fields."

UMBC Women's Basketball, 1968

This Belongs to Royce Bradshaw '70*, Political Science

Early Support for the Cause

In spring 1968, predominantly black Bowie State College staged a student strike, claiming that black colleges were underfunded, and that their physical plant was in very bad shape. Several of us at UMBC decided that their problems affected all the colleges and universities in Maryland and that we should support them. We contacted all the student governments in Maryland, and asked them to attend a meeting at UMBC.

Almost all public colleges in Maryland were represented. As it was a racial issue, there was AP, UPI and other national press at the meeting. This was probably the first time that UMBC got national press attention. During the meeting we got a message that Dr. Martin Luther King had just been assassinated. We suspended the meeting. We met about a month later, at UMBC, and formed the United Colleges of Maryland. We organized a march in Annapolis. We asked students to dress and act responsibly, to show that we were carrying out our rights as responsible citizens.

Over 800 students from 13 state colleges and universities attended. A small group of us met with Governor Spiro Agnew, who later became Richard Nixon's vice-president. We had several editorials published in local newspapers, including one for WJZ-TV, which they entitled, "The Right Kind of Protest". This effort generated a lot of good publicity for UMBC. Dr. Kuhn and the faculty were very supportive. We were recognized and supported by the Maryland Council for Higher Education.

The Unique Gift to UMBC by the Founding Class

It has been the tradition, at many colleges, for the graduating class to give a gift to their school. The first UMBC seniors wanted to make sure that they gave a gift of value that would start a precedent to continue for many years. A student committee decided that we should raise monies for a loan fund to provide assistance to students who were faced with family emergencies.

A goal was set for $10,000. The funds would be raised by asking businesses and corporations to donate. The seniors would "earn" this contribution by doing a community/charitable project on behalf of the benefactor. So, for one donation, a company would help university students and the community. It was a win-win public relations project for them.

After getting endorsement letters from the chancellor, the governor, our senators and the financial aid officer, the class sent correspondence to a number of corporations. The student committee then met with them. The response was fantastic, and a total of $13,000 was raised, exceeding our goal by $3,000. The two biggest donors were Carling Brewing Company and the Baltimore Colts.

Replies were received from numerous corporations, informing us that they had already spent their charitable gifts budget for the year, but praising the effort as unique and inspiring.

The graduating class of 1970 did painting and maintenance work at the School of the Chimes and several Community Action Agencies. Almost fifty percent of the senior class participated in these projects. The founding class is very proud of UMBC and its growth and stature in the academic community. Unfortunately with growth comes even greater needs. We would encourage all classes to continue what we started, either as a class, or individually, to support our school and students as they aspire to make a significant contribution to our society.

After UMBC:

- Studied Political Science at College Park
- Served as Graduate Assistant to Dr. Albin O. Kuhn, started Alumni and Development program at UMBC
- Elected President of the Maryland Chapter of the American Society for Public Administration, 1975
- Worked at all levels of government: UMBC, Baltimore City, Maryland Department of Human Resources, Social Security Administration, and NATO in Belgium.
- Served 25 years in NATO, including Bosnia and Afghanistan.
- Married, 11 grandchildren
- "My time at NATO was the highlight of my career."

*Royce actually completed his degree requirements in 1969, but there was no Commencement until June 1970.

Senior Service Project, 1970

This Belongs to Kathy Oliver Brauer, Sandy Muha Perry, Phil Perry, and Glen Besa '72, History (Kathy)

The Environmental Defense Coalition and UMBC Reclamation Center

In the early 70s at the dawn of the environmental movement and the first Earth Day, the UMBC Reclamation Center was operated by the campus-based student organization, the Environmental Defense Coalition (EDC), and was the hub of environmental activism on campus and in the greater community. Originally founded by a group of graduating seniors, led by Brian Kahntroff, as a trial project, after their graduation EDC was passed down to other students. Our EDC faculty advisors, Dr. Robert Burchard and Dr. David Lewis, actively supported our efforts, and personally used and occasionally volunteered at the recycling center with their wives. Our committee also collaborated with the New Democratic Coalition, an organization also coordinated by former UMBC students.

Consisting of separate dumpsters for cans and different color glass bottles and jars as well as a trailer for newspapers, this recycling center was one of the biggest in Maryland at a time before local government sponsored curbside recycling. Ironically at the time glass was our most valuable product while today that market has all but disappeared. There was very little plastic back then and just like now most plastic was not and is not recycled. At one point Dr. Burchard coordinated a meeting of our committee with Baltimore County Councilman Gary Huddles and Charles Farley, head of the Bureau of Sanitation, where we pushed for Baltimore County to develop recycling centers county wide. Recycling at the county level was an idea well before its time.

Officially open year round on Saturdays and Sundays, the center was staffed by student, faculty and community volunteers. The operations consisted of taking recyclable materials that had been dropped off by the community and throwing glass bottles against the side of the dumpsters to break and compact the glass. Users of the center were asked to clean their recyclables and to crush their cans before they dropped them off at the center. Most did just that but who knew that yellow jackets love beer? The steady buzz of yellow jackets around the brown glass dumpster in the summer and fall informed us that some beer bottles weren't quite empty when brought to the center and placed in the dumpster. When dumpsters or the trailer were full, the volunteer student director of the center would call Brooklyn Salvage to come pick up the full containers and replace them with empties that we would again fill up with cans, glass and newspapers. Another member recalls volunteering in the winter when on occasion newspapers left outside the trailer would get wet and freeze together into heavy blocks of newsprint popsicles.

Unique among student clubs and organizations at UMBC at the time, the reclamation center actually generated money, several thousand dollars annually, which the Administration managed and approved the use of by EDC volunteers for environmental programs and causes on campus and in the community. EDC even had a small office on the top floor of the Hillcrest building on top of the hill on campus. In the days before computers and Xerox machines, we had a typewriter and an old hand cranked Ditto machine that we used to produce a newsletter and environmental guide that we distributed on campus and to patrons of the reclamation center on weekends. Among the many programs sponsored by EDC, one memorable one was bringing Ralph Nader to speak at the campus when he was an early and prominent consumer and environmental advocate. Other committee activities involved working to clean up Patapsco State Park, planting trees, lobbying the state legislature, contributing financially to other local environmental organizations and hosting monthly meetings with speakers on various environmental topics.

Some of our members went on to be elementary school teachers who incorporated environmental lessons into their school programs and classroom instruction. Another went on to make environmental activism a professional career working with the Sierra Club. Our work with EDC and the reclamation center instilled a lifelong environmental ethic in many of the volunteers and community members that lasts to this day.

After UMBC:

- Taught for 40 years in the fields of special education and computer technology
- Married with 1 child, 1 grandchild
- Active in political campaigns and teacher association activities
- Active in local community and environmental education programs
- Retired and enjoys genealogy research (History major came in handy!)

This Belongs to Wayne N. Bushell '71, Physics

Catching the Right Bus

Many of my early memories of UMBC involve getting there and back home. UMBC was a commuter school for the first few years. The entire student population arrived each morning (or afternoon depending on your class schedule) and departed each evening after classes concluded. A few of the students, myself included, commuted by way of the MTA buses. After riding the #19 from the Hamilton area, I would transfer to the #3 line in downtown Baltimore which would drop us off at the intersection of Linden Avenue and Shelbourne Rd. You had to get the "Maiden Choice" bus and not the "Leeds Ave" bus or your walk was a lot longer. After that we walked along Shelbourne Rd to Poplar Ave where we followed the asphalt paved pathway that paralleled Poplar Ave until we got to the campus. Some of us had our first classes of the day (at 8AM) in the old Hillcrest Administration building, so we continued the walk by climbing the hill to the building that used to be part of the Spring Grove hospital.

The walk along what was essentially a golf-cart path and over the small wooden bridge was sometimes enjoyable and sometimes not so much. During the first few weeks of classes, the weather was pleasant and the fields along the road were heavily infested with grasshoppers, which seemed to love hitching a ride on the walkers. As the weather turned colder and nastier, the walk obviously was less enjoyable.

Time between classes was usually spent in the cafeteria meeting with and making new friends, trying to finish up some homework or grabbing a snack from the vending machines. There were really only 3 buildings, besides Hillcrest, they were the Gym/Cafeteria, Lecture Hall, and Academic building which housed the regular classrooms, chemistry, bio and language labs, Library and faculty offices. Hillcrest housed the administration, some classrooms and offices and after a while the Rathskeller was added. At the end of the day of classes, the return walk back to the bus stop lugging a load of textbooks and notebooks always seemed even longer.

Less than a year after graduating with my degree in Physics, I returned to UMBC to work as a Research Tech in the Biology department for about 5 more years. There are many other memories of the years at UMBC, but the walk back and forth to the bus stop really sticks in my memory.

After UMBC:

- Worked as a Research Assistant at UMBC for Marty Schwartz for five years.
- Worked with a software developer at Aberdeen Proving Grounds. Spent 40 years at APG as a Program Manager, Software Engineer, and Instructor.

- Married Claudette four days after graduation (it was a busy week!) and still married after 51 years. One daughter Grace and granddaughter Meika
- "I continue to do some consulting when it doesn't interfere with golf."

Many UMBC Students' Mode of Transportation

This Belongs to Patricia Callan '72, History

A Library Story

As a member of the UMBC class of 1972, I struggled to find a job after graduation. I applied to the State and Federal government but I was told most of the jobs were going to returning Vietnam vets first. Then a friend from UMBC told me about a clerical job at the UMBC Library. I applied and got the job in the Accounting and Receiving department with a '70 alum as my boss (Linda Lyall Sowers). To this day, it is still the best job experience in my 30 years with the University of Maryland. The campus was new, the faculty enthused and inspiring and the young library with a new boss fit right into the infectious energy. The Head Librarian wanted all who entered the library to feel like they had had the best service and all of us played a part in their experience. That included those who worked the front desks and those behind the scenes. He wanted us to greet each person warmly and give any assistance they might need. Every day, each staff member had to file cards in the card catalog for an hour a day; that included librarians, clerks, secretaries, and the boss himself. He rewarded our efforts throughout the year by allowing us to throw parties when the school closed for winter and summer breaks. We organized a champagne brunch that we catered ourselves (we had some fabulous cooks on staff -Did I mention that we self-published two Library Cookbooks?), we had a Summer Olympic games on the field outside the library with tug of war, bag races and lots of laughing, cheering and fun. We hosted a roast of our fearless leader, we performed in skits, and we held a Gong-show-like talent show. At Halloween, most Library staff dressed in costume to the delight of students and faculty alike. Our boss joined in and arrived to work in a handmade Mickey Mouse costume. We decorated for Christmas and wore green on St. Patrick's Day.

There was a true feeling of camaraderie amongst this young-at-heart staff. We were a team. We worked together to move the books ourselves when the new section of the library opened. We helped each other by understanding each other's jobs, in case we needed to help with a backlog. We did the work with energy, joy, and a sense of duty and that made this the best place to work, bar none.

After UMBC:

- Worked for thirty years for the University of Maryland (UMBC, UMMS, UMUC, UMBI, UMCP).
- I'm retired and traveling the world as much as I can.
- "Dr. Storch and Dr. Sherwin inspired me, and instilled in me an interest in the ancient cities."

This Belongs to Joan Costello '73, Social Work

Smokey Robinson

First semester in college after 12 years of parochial school. It was a new world with its own language - standard deviation, bell curve, median. I had signed up for Statistics to take care of a Math and Sociology requirement with one course. Then there were other strange sayings from Professor Robinson like horseshoe guess. Can't remember other "Robinsonisms", but I will never forget that he smoked in class and regularly got the chalk and cigarette interchanged - at least, he smoked the chalk but didn't put the cigarette out by writing on the board! It was quite a show. I didn't get that math requirement as I didn't make it within the bell curve or benefit enough from grading on a curve. Welcome to college!

The UMBC campus was quite a team endeavor - family members worked in different departments on campus and still do, graduates stayed and worked for a while, some for a long while, still do. There were a number of folks who graduated from the first classes who began their full time work adventures at UMBC, like Trish Callan '72, Louie (Linda) Lyall Sowers '70, Deborah Tinsley Cosby '71, Mary Felber-Blum '71, Mary Ogle Huebner '73 (Mary did begin classes in 1970, took a little break to work in the Library, after graduating she worked in the Business Office), Simmona Simmons '74, was one of the first employees in the Library in 1966 and just retired in 2013. We all worked in the Library and 4 became librarians. Simmona headed Circulation in the Library in the beginning and started taking classes also, serving as a Reference Librarian for many years. The growing up, cooperation and shenanigans formed bonds that have lasted to the present.

I started as a student employee in 1970 and they put me in the Head Librarian's office. When it took me hours to finish a memo - remember, no computers to easily make changes, carbon copies, thank god I had taken personal typing as a high school club activity or who knows how long it would have taken - they decided to move me to the Record and Tape Library. I stayed there for a while eventually becoming the supervisor. Later the Library inherited Audio Visual Services from Education and I became its supervisor and later the coordinator of the International Media Center (the language lab). I grew up with UMBC, working there 41 years as a full time employee after 3 years as a student employee. Crossed paths with many student employees, faculty and staff and enjoyed meeting every one of them and was exposed to many different cultures and dreams of these students - it was all good. I remember a lecturer from Slovakia remarking that he was so tired at the end of the day having to think in a different language all day - it never occurred to me. A student worker from Iran was sent to the US for schooling to avoid being sent to the army and war - I couldn't imagine leaving my family at 18 and coming to a foreign land and making my way. I admired him - 2 younger brothers joined him as they hit that magic age. They became a pharmacist and two dentists.

Other workers from the Founding Four classes included:
Bob Dietrich '70 worked in Biology for 31 years in labs and eventually building manager; family ties - his mother worked in History.

David Servary '71 Economics - he worked elsewhere but joined UMBC staff later

Thornton McIver (Mac) '72 Economics

Frank Porter '72 History, eventually became a UMBC professor

George Vitak '72 Biology was a student worker in Central receiving, full time in Facilities Planning, then supervisor of telecommunication services and finally as Director of campus card and mail services and retired after 38 years in 2011. In George's bio he mentioned that the Library Pond was designed by RTKL Architects and is filled by a man made stream carrying runoff down the hill from boilers in UMBC's Central Plant. "RTKL Architects made that into one of the distinguishing architectural features of the campus," he says of the pond. "We used to have tug of wars across it."

Eugenie Vitak '73 Biology, met George in Genetics and formed a lifelong bond. Genie later worked 20 years as Library staff, unfortunately, she passed away in 2020. Two of their daughters were also connected to UMBC, one as a student and the other a visiting professor.

Bryan MacKay '73 BS, '79 MS instructor in Biology, retired as Senior Lecturer after 44 consecutive years with UMBC, his mother worked in the Business office. Bryan has written six popular guidebooks to outdoor activities and nature, including "A Year across Maryland: A Week by Week Guide to Discovering Nature in the Chesapeake Region"

Jim Milani '73 worked 45 years spanning academic advising and counseling to administrative affairs and finance. At his death in June 2019, he was the Assistant Dean of Administration and Operations in the College of Engineering. Jim was one of the most enthusiastic, caring, involved people I knew at UMBC.

After UMBC:

- Worked at UMBC until 2014 in media areas - Library, AV Services, Multimedia Center
- Enjoys nieces and nephews and now "greats"
- Enjoys quilting, ushering at Baltimore Theatres, mahjongg, UMBC Theatre and Men's Basketball
- Member of The Wisdom Institute (UMBC retirees)
- Lives in Catonsville

This Belongs to Linda Sorace Crites '72, Sociology

Pardon My French

After graduating from Western High School in Baltimore City in 1968, I had few options for college because of my family's lack of resources. Fortunately, UMBC had just been established two years earlier, two and a half miles from my home in Yale Heights. Based on my Western records I received a State Senatorial Scholarship to go there. Having had 6 years of French, I tested out of the first three semesters of French and was in a fourth semester French class taught strictly in French by a lovely, native French professor, Genevieve Smith.

At that time the legal drinking age for beer was 18 and I turned 18 just as the Fall 1968 semester began. While I didn't believe that I would single-handedly turn UMBC into a party school, I was more than willing to do my part to help that along. Some of you early alumni may remember a pizza joint on Route 40 called Pappy's Pizza. And what's a pizza place without beer, which they served in very large steins. As a rather small person (5 feet tall, 100 pounds), a stein was quite enough to give me a good buzz.

Well, one particular Thursday, I decided to go to Pappy's for "lunch" with some friends. It still astonishes me that I actually went back to UMBC after pizza and beer to go to my French class. While my knowledge of French was pretty good, my pronunciation and accent were somewhat less than perfect.

So here I am in French class and the professor asks me a question in her very native French. Sadly, I don't remember what the question was. (Maybe because of the buzz.) Without any hesitation, the correct answer in the most perfect French accent simply rolled right out of me. Looking completely wide-eyed and shocked, she responded in English, "Why don't you always speak like that?"

While I may not have single-handedly made UMBC a party school, I did my part as best I could, and maybe improved my French grade in the process!

After UMBC:

- Worked for Social Security Administration 1973-1976
- Received degrees from University of Maryland School of Social Work, MSW, 1978, Ph.D., 1988
- 1978-1993, worked as a Social Worker providing supportive services, conducting research, and HHS grant administration for families of children with developmental disabilities at U of MD Medical School, City Head Start, Assn for the Care of Children's Health.
- 1993, began private practice as a Clinical Social Worker providing psychotherapy to individuals, couples and families in Columbia, MD
- Met Jim Crites 1978, married Jim and his kids, Wendy and Travis 1979
- 2008 Moved to Marriottsville, in Carroll County where I am still in private practice

This Belongs to Kenneth Diehl '70, Psychology

The Road Almost Not Travelled

Two weeks before the start of my first college semester in 1966 I was taking my first ever drive up Wilkens Avenue on a hot summer day. I was heading to Catonsville Community College to apply for enrollment. The prior seven weeks had been an emotional nightmare. I had turned down acceptances and opportunities to play baseball at the University of Kentucky and Ohio State. All of this in response to an offer of a full ride scholarship to the University of North Carolina NROTC program. Subsequently my physician's medical form error, ascribing a non-existent history of asthma, led to the loss of the UNC scholarship. Hence my enrollment at "Cate State" instead of Ohio State. That summer day I saw a sign for UMBC. I honestly had no prior awareness of UMBC, or what it was. Continuing up Wilkens Avenue I saw a silo on the property and concluded that UMBC was an agricultural school. Most likely a place to study cows*.

Two relatively non-challenging years later I was again accepted at Kentucky and Ohio State. Reversal of family fortunes again led me to decline the offers rather late in the college application process. What to do? Well I guess I'll go study cows.

The first time I saw UMBC it was unsettling. Barren, isolated, austere, devoid of charm and character. Sterile. It looked like something a Junior Partner architect had sketched on a lunch napkin five minutes before his presentation. Add a barbed wire fence and a guard post and it could have been an annex of NSA. Even the cows were hiding. The fall of '68 was brutal. I disliked everything about the University. I mean everything. Classmates likely referred to me as a sphincter. Although I'm sure they used a different word. Adding insult to injury I arrived at my parked car one day to find a parking ticket. I had been parking at this same dead end road for five weeks. Then one day while I am in class they erect a No Parking sign and gave me a ticket. Lovely.

My transformation began in November of '68. Despite my Psych/Pre-Med ambitions I was intrigued by the notice of a Study Abroad course. Three exceptional educators led the expedition to England, Rome and France. Drs. Sherwin, Freyman and Storch provided what I would years later view as a life changing experience. Hands on experience with thousands of years of history and culture, combined with ample sampling of the fine Italian Sangiovese grapes enhanced the expert instruction. I met and enjoyed a wonderful group of funny, down to earth fellow students. We went to war together and formed a strong bond. The experience was so meaningful that I joined the same group of profs in a study abroad trip to England, Greece, and Austria the following year. Upon returning from Europe baseball season was beginning. Everything is right in the world during baseball season. I was familiar with several of the players having played against them over the years. Here is a trivia question for you. Who was the losing pitcher in UMBC's first ever baseball victory? Me. UMBC won 3-1. I pitched a five hitter for CCC and we made five errors.

The Fall of 1969 began promisingly. Challenging courses and dynamic professors. Coping with the physical image of the campus became easier. I learned that if I stayed inside one of the two academic buildings I didn't have to look at the campus. Outside I would just look through one eye and squint. Finally dorms were constructed. Somehow they even managed to make them look austere and resemble a local Elementary School. With the support of Dr. Ken Ellis (Psychology) and Dr. Robert Burchard (Biology) my research into hormonal levels and dominant behavior in rats was facilitated. The highlight of the fall semester of my Senior Year was performing testicular surgery on 24 male rats from 8 PM until 9 AM the next morning. There's a skill set that doesn't widely generalize to society.

As a member of UMBC's first graduating class the spring semester of '70 dawned with hope and promise. That second trip to Europe and my final year of college baseball were eagerly anticipated. However, Semester Interruptus had other plans. The pall of the Vietnam War and racial injustice hung over the campus like a cloud of industrial pollution. Focusing on course work was increasingly difficult as greater concerns about the country and the world began to take over. Increasing campus unrest reached a tipping point following the Kent State massacre. Suddenly my semester was prematurely cancelled. We were given the option of either taking a Final Exam, or use our existent course grade and sent packing. My undergrad experience ended like it began, frustrating and unfulfilling. Graduation ceremonies were held in the open area adjacent to what was then the Union Building. Noted news anchorman Howard K. Smith was the commencement speaker. That warm June day was more about perspiration rather than inspiration. His words felt hollow and irrelevant. The graduation felt meaningless. I knew prior that I was heading to Baylor University to pursue my Doctorate in Clinical Psych. I remarked to a friend that day that I finally experienced my favorite vista of UMBC- in my rear view mirror.

The next 15 years were a blur. Grad school, Clinic, Internship, Doctoral Electives at the University of Maryland Medical School, a Post-Doc in Boston, and setting up my practice. One day while again traveling in Europe I inexplicably began to reflect upon my experiences at UMBC. For years I had stressed to my High School Senior patients that what they learned about themselves in college was more important than what they would learn in any course. Curiously I had never considered that possibility myself. I realized that at UMBC I had not only learned time management and how to study, I also learned perseverance and how to fully commit to a goal. This was very different from just talking about what my plans were. Shrugging off my adolescent narcissism as it were. The research I had been so graciously funded and easily facilitated by Drs. Ellis and Burchard helped me to understand research design, journal research and analytical thinking (not to mention scrotum surgery and rat castration). My two trips to Europe with the Ancient Studies Department were transformative in so many ways. In retrospect I seriously doubt that I would have had these exceptional experiences at either of the Universities I had declined to attend. UMBC was exactly where I needed to be and I am grateful for the role the University played in my success. The fact that UMBC was new and reasonably flexible allowed me to customize my education to my unique goals.

Epilogue. Ten years ago several of my baseball teammates and I were invited back to campus to speak to the ball players and their families. Sort of an Antiques Roadshow. This was my first trip back to campus in 40 years. Wow. Suddenly there was a full blown University where a cow pasture previously existed. Quite impressive. As sort of a revenge it took me 45 minutes to locate the designated building. Forty years ago you could walk through every building on campus in less than thirty minutes. It was satisfying to see the evolution of the University. But the age old question remains. Where are they keeping the cows?*

*Actually, there were never cows on the land that would become UMBC.

After UMBC:

- Attended Baylor University 70-75, graduated with Doctorate in Clinical Psychology.
- Completed Doctoral electives at University of Maryland Medical School in Neurology and Neuropathology, 73-74. Completed Post-Doctoral Fellowship at Tufts-New England Medical Center in Neuropsychology 75-76.
- Outstanding Contribution to Public Service Award from Division 18 of the American Psychological Association 1980.
- Opened Private Practice 1981 to present.
- Helped three Brain Injury Units open and get accredited in metropolitan Baltimore area late 70s and 80s
- International speaker on mental health needs of incarcerated individuals.80-82.
- Staff member, Johns Hopkins Hospital 75-80.
- National Expert Witness in the area of Neuropsychology and malingering 76-present.
- Adjunct Professor, Loyola University 93-95. Helped Loyola Psychology Department acquire accreditation.
- Married Barbara Surosky, Loyola University, 1983 to present. Son born 1990 - Web Designer and manager of internet sales for wine distributor. Daughter born 1993 - Travel Nurse, currently residing in Belgium.

This Belongs to Bob Dietrich '70, Biological Sciences

We Were a Team!

It seemed like the flyers were everywhere: "Anyone interested in playing lacrosse attend this meeting". I had never picked up a lacrosse stick in my life but always liked the beauty when it was played properly. Also, Maryland was one of the hotbeds of the sport and it should be the state sport (It's Jousting!).

So I went to the meeting and found a bunch of guys who expressed an interest. Some had played lacrosse at Baltimore area schools - Calvert Hall, Loyola, City College HS, Poly, and a number of public schools. Del Langdon, who worked in the Admissions Department was running the meeting. His enthusiasm, and welcoming put everyone at ease. He said it didn't matter if you had played before because his ultimate goal was to teach the game.

So off we went; picked up our equipment (helmet, gloves and stick) and began practicing scooping, throwing, and shooting. At that time all of the lacrosse sticks were made out of wood, leather and catgut made by native North Americans in Canada. They were temperamental to keep aligned and sagged in the rain. Coach Langdon was a great teacher and motivator. After a couple of weeks things started to look good, not great, with the experienced players showing us inexperienced players how it was done. We were a team!

The first years we played our games right in the Quad (the outdoor pool had not been built yet). We played some of the local Community Colleges and University "B" teams. We won more than we lost during the next three years and became a close-knit group of players.

After UMBC:

- Worked in biomedical research for 1.5 years at JHU and UMB
- Worked for 40 years in the UMBC Biological Sciences Department as Lab Prep and Facilities Manager.
- Married Mimi Haw, class of 1970, in August 1970
- Volunteered with Catonsville Recreation and Parks Lacrosse Program, 25 years
- Boy Scout Leader, Troop 456 Catonsville, 30 years
- Has 2 sons and 4 grandchildren, lives in Catonsville.
- Retired in 2011 and volunteers as a Bicycle Ranger in Patapsco Valley State Park

This Belongs to Mimi Haw Dietrich '70, American Studies

The Pioneer

There's something about the word "Pioneer" that's exciting. In 1966, or maybe it was 1965, I heard that there was going to be a new university in Maryland, just a few miles from my house in Catonsville. I remember my high school advisor saying the students in the first class at UMBC would be Pioneers!

Yes, I would be a brave pioneer. Honestly, it sounded fabulous because it was so close to home, in my comfort zone. After all, Towson was on the other side of Baltimore, and College Park was far away. I had never been to either place! And those colleges were rumored to be so big, with thousands of students in huge lecture halls. My education so far had been the Catholic school at St. Mark one mile from my house, and the all-girls Catholic high school, IND in Baltimore city. I walked two blocks in my neighborhood to get on the bus to go there.

UMBC sounded like a perfect adventure to this pioneer.

Growing up, I went everywhere with friends. But on the first day at UMBC, I felt very alone as I stood in line by myself. It rained. The sidewalks weren't finished and we walked on plywood boards. I had to talk to strangers! There were boys in the registration line! So much was happening at once, and we moved from line to line to meet advisors, choose classes, sign up, get an ID card, buy books, and start our overwhelming pioneer adventures!

One of my most memorable UMBC first-semester experiences occurred in the lobby of the multipurpose building gym. A group of Jewish students started to dance the Hora. Remember….I went to 12 years of Catholic School during the dark ages when it was frowned upon to talk to anyone not Catholic. I'll never forget the moment when Michael Sandler took my hand and invited me to dance. That moment changed my life. He opened my eyes to a world I had never known, to the world with all kinds of people I had never experienced. This for me was the moment that this pioneer stepped out of her comfort zone and UMBC became a university.

Now in the UMBC Commons (the exact site of that memorable dance), there are flags flying for all of the students' countries. It's a beautiful sight, but even more awesome as you realize how UMBC has grown, from those first years with pioneer students from all over the city, to students now from all over the world.

Thank you, Dr. Sherwin

I wonder if UMBC created the MiniMester?

The cold weeks in January were traditionally a time to rest and recuperate from the fall semester and get ready for the challenge of spring semester. But in 1968, UMBC scheduled a special session in January and challenged the professors to teach courses that were condensed into three weeks, usually awarding 1-3 credits and covering a wide variety of topics.

Thinking back, the best part of MiniMester for students, was that it was a special time to sign up for only one course, concentrate on it, and experience a class in a different way. For many of us, it was much more relaxed, and what we experienced was education for the pure enjoyment of learning!

In 1968, Dr. Jones taught The American Student, a course designed to familiarize the students at our young UMBC with a variety of students and other universities. On the most memorable day, he invited our moms to come and sit in on the class in the lecture hall. We learned that our moms were very interested in what we were learning!

In my house, we often thank Dr. Sherwin for a MiniMester class in Scientific Terminology, Latin and Greek Roots. My husband Bob loved that MiniMester class! Not only did it help in his Biology degree, but it still enables him to answer some strange Jeopardy questions. When he comes up with correct obscure answers, we look at each other and just say, "Thanks, Dr. Sherwin!"

My favorite MiniMester class was a 1969 Ancient Studies trip to Rome, London and Paris. Drs. Sherwin, Storch, and Freyman took 40 students to study abroad. We traveled and experienced the ancient ruins of Rome, art in Florence, discos in London, and escargot in Paris. Our one assignment was to keep a journal-mine is full of details, places, and fun experiences. I recently discovered that my friend Larry Wilder still reads his during January each year! During that MiniMester class I spent my 21st birthday at a dinner in Rome, was gifted with a love of travel, and learned so much about myself in those three magical weeks.

"Good Morning, UMBC!"

When UMBC opened in 1966, most of the offices were on the fourth floor of the Academic Building. As you got off the elevator on the fourth floor, you passed a small room containing the telephone switchboard, the communications center for the entire campus. Ceil Nedeloff worked at the switchboard, answering all incoming phone calls with a cheery "Good Morning, UMBC!" She connected outgoing long distance calls, provided "information" and was truly the voice of the university at 301-455-1000.

I was one of Ceil's work-study students, giving her a break in between my classes. Because the switchboard room was next to the elevator, Ceil's office became a gathering space for students who worked in the offices on the fourth floor. They would often stop to say hello and visit, resting on the old comfortable green sofa, the only piece of furniture in her office.

Ceil was not just a fabulous boss, she was our campus mom. We confided in her and she listened to our problems about classes, boyfriend issues, and guided us through many social catastrophes. She taught us business etiquette and professionalism, as we interacted with outside callers, campus professors, administrators and staff. Her friendliness and respect for everyone was infectious and she taught me to interact with adults in a way I never had before. Those of us who worked on the switchboard spent many hours getting advice from Ceil. Some of the best life lessons I learned at UMBC were not from professors, but from our delightful telephone operator, Ceil.

"The Concert"

Growing up in the 60's, I loved music and concerts. I saw The Beatles, Bob Dylan, and The Supremes at the Baltimore Civic Center. But the best concert I ever attended was at UMBC on April 22, 1967, as part of the first UMBC Spring Week. Otis Redding, "The King of Soul", performed in Gym 1, accompanied by his twelve piece band. He performed two forty-five minute sets. The tickets were $5 and it was semi-formal. It really wasn't a concert like we think of today in large stadiums. It was more intimate with everyone dancing in the small gym, we were so close to the band! We danced all night.

I don't remember what I wore that night, I remember going with a group of friends, and I remember the excitement of a big name concert coming to UMBC. Otis wrote Respect in 1965, so I'm sure that was a highlight! We all seem to remember that he sang Sittin' on the Dock of the Bay, but research confirms that he didn't write that song until 6 months later! He recorded it in December 1967 just before his untimely death at 26 in a plane crash.

Any time we talk about The Concert, I immediately remember the soft sounds of Otis Redding's voice, the loud brass music, the energy of the dancing students, and our little Gym 1 transformed into a huge concert experience I will never forget.

Teacher! Teacher!

Honestly, when I graduated from UMBC, I was done, finished and ready to go. I was a student teacher my last semester and I was ready to fly! It wasn't until many years later that I realized the true value of my four years at UMBC.

I was a math major for one semester, until Calculus. I was a Spanish major until I had to read an entire book written in Spanish. I struggled through a Speech class with Miss Lynch, until I finally learned to stop giggling. I already knew I was not a scientist, but I loved history and literature. Eventually my classes and friends led me to American Studies. It was a perfect interdisciplinary mix of topics I loved.

I had enough Literature classes to qualify for a teaching certificate and graduated to teach English at a Baltimore county junior high. In 1966, I signed a contract with the State of Maryland, promising to teach in Maryland and they promised to pay my $200 tuition per semester.

My most valuable UMBC class was an education seminar with Dr. Neville. I learned to use behavioral objectives to focus on what I was teaching and measure students' progress. The seminar involved an amazing experience (remember this was 1969) of filming us as we taught classes. Seeing myself say "you know" and "ummm" too many times, taught me to speak slowly and carefully and changed my life!

My path as a teacher led me to adventures with middle schoolers, preschoolers, and adults. The education classes I took at UMBC and Dr. Neville's guidance, gave me the confidence to teach anything, so I made a career out of teaching what I love.

After the American Bicentennial in 1976, I fell in love with quilts. Patchwork pieces that fit together like geometric puzzles (remember that math major) led me to some very special historical quilts in Baltimore. I loved the process of making quilts and started teaching classes at a local quilt shop. One of those classes (I recorded the class to give me the basic outline) led to writing a book about finishing quilts.

That book led to teaching quilting on a national level. I traveled to quilt guilds all over the country, taught on Quilting Cruises to Alaska and New England, taught at the International Quilt Festival in Houston, and my favorite classes are still local classes about Baltimore Album Quilts.

In 2013 I was named the Teacher of the Year by Professional Quilter magazine, and honored by the Quilters Hall of Fame in 2015. I even taught an American Studies class about quilting and history at UMBC.

In 2019 my quilts were displayed at the Maryland Historical Society in my Hometown Girl exhibit. I felt honored to have my quilts hanging next to inspirational historical quilts made in Baltimore in the 1850's.

My favorite UMBC class was the 1968 MiniMester Ancient Studies class, an incredible trip to London, Rome, and Paris. It was the highlight of my UMBC education. It was my first flight. The professors, the students, the international experiences certainly inspired a life-long love of travel! UMBC took me to places I never thought I'd see!

Thinking back…..my experience as a Math major helped me understand how to make quilts. My American Studies major combined Literature, Writing, History, Sociology, Material Culture, and a wonderful mixture of topics. My study abroad trip to Rome gave me a confidence to travel by myself. Add that to the confidence I learned about teaching at UMBC, and I feel I can trace my life experiences right back to my UMBC education!

After UMBC:

- Married Bob Dietrich, UMBC 1970
- Taught middle school, pre-school, and adults for 50 years
- Was inducted into The Quilters Hall of Fame, 2015
- Received the UMBC Alumni Award for Distinguished Service, 2018
- Exhibited her Hometown Girl quilts at the Maryland Historical Society, 2019
- Lives in Catonsville and enjoys spending time with her family: sons Jon and Ryan, their wives, and four grandchildren.

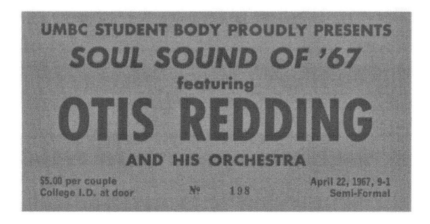

Otis Redding Concert Ticket

This Belongs to Phillip Douglas '72, History

Down to Earth

When I attended UMBC, I had already served 4 years in the Army, worked a year, and went to Anne Arundel Community College for a year. So I concentrated on graduating after a total of 3 years of college. UMBC was and is a wonderful college that I have been forever grateful to for my education and proud to call my Alma Mater. We still had the old house on the hill, a silo, the library was just built and dorms as well. It's where I experienced the first official "Earth Day".

The Long Plywood Walk to the Library

This Belongs to Edward Damian Doyle '70, Psychology

Cheeseburger...Cheeseburger

We all have memories of our years at UMBC. For some, we met our life long partner and fully engaged our culture in the decades to follow for our families, country and beyond! And then there are the 'others' like the famous cheeseburger in the cafeteria vending machines. At first we had small infrared ovens to heat our food that were efficient but 'slow'. One day the microwave ovens appeared to warm up our cheeseburgers FAST! I had long noticed that the cheese never seemed to melt. There were a few of us sharing lunch when I asked the question at what temperature would the cheese on my hamburger melt?

With no thermometer in hand but a good sense of temperature, I placed my cheeseburger in the new microwave and set it to 'HIGH' Rapidly - it heated, after a few minutes, a small flame appeared on the corner of the cheeseburger bun. The small flame gradually encircled the cheese – encrusting the bun. It went on and on! I removed it all safely and "THE CHEESE – NEVER MELTED"!
It was not the greatest food but we liked it for the good times spent together and friendships made that have lasted a lifetime.

Touched by an Angel

It was the fall of 1969, I was still in need of my freshman English requirement. I had been unable to complete the course after many tries. I am down to almost my last opportunity to complete this requirement in order to graduate. I found myself reading my first book ever, written by Emile Zola, 'L'Assommoir'. The lessons learned from his novel are with me always. I would spend hours and days on what seemed like an endless journey, as each page was taking almost a half hour. I had some sense of my learning disability; however, with little understanding of its real dynamics. It was a matter of page to eye coordination. I eventually read every word but dropped the course, for a reason that I no longer remember. I had developed my own methods of learning and I needed a style of lecturing and detailed class participation. My class notes were recorded in a personal stenographic shorthand with Latin notation in sophisticated detail. These notes became my textbooks. My textbooks were of little help, yet I purchased and cherished them.

Now it is the Spring of 1970 and I still do not have my English requirement. Registration is about to close. There is something even more pressing. Sharyn and I are engaged, a wedding in the Fall. Two to four times every day I would walk to the registrar's office, hoping to find a course to complete my English requirement - all the courses were full. As the last hour of the last day was rapidly approaching - the registrar informed me that a course had just opened one slot an hour ago. It was taught by Dr. Arnquist and I knew that I could learn from him, as I had done so before. It was as if an Angel had reached down and touched me. I can recall that moment with a deep passionate recall, as I left Hillcrest in joyful tears to return to campus. And then, it came together as I had always hoped.

Every day I use many of life's lessons that I learned in his courses and through the treasured literature of the ages.

After UMBC:

- Worked as a Juvenile Counselor starting in 1970
- Earned Master's degree and became supervisor of Juvenile Counselors
- Loved technology and became Medical Care Specialist 1990
- Worked until retirement 1999.
- Married Sharyn Doyle, class of 1970, in November of 1970
- Lives in Catonsville, near son who graduated from UMBC Honors College and is currently the Deputy CIO and Senior Associate VP in the Division of Information Technology at UMBC
- Enjoys watching grandson grow and learning to drive as a sophomore in high school.
- Currently volunteers with Seniors on technology assistance.

Gourmet Food for Everyone on Demand!

This Belongs to Sharyn Faye Miller Doyle '70, Social Sciences

Inspirational Faculty

My best memory was of meeting my future husband Ed at UMBC. Next were the many professors that I had.

There were many psychology courses I needed to take to fulfill teaching certification requirements, yet we couldn't major in education at that time. Therefore, psychology was my next best option. Most of the courses were taught by Professor Janice Goldberg and I did not prefer her style of teaching…yet what could I do. Dr. Henley came on staff later and I enjoyed her many courses.

We could only minor in Education and there were 6 of us that did so with Dr. Janet Carsetti. All of us completed student teaching in Anne Arundel County and all of us became specialists and later school administrators…all staying in A. A. County.

I took a genetics class and it was fantastic with Dr. Snope. I had the opportunity to visit leaders of several different religious institutions and interview them on eugenics. Wow….talk about different philosophies!

Dr. Arnquist who taught American Studies was dynamic and under appreciated by other faculty. Dr. Groninger, who was wheel chair bound, taught statistics and advanced math related classes. Back in 1966 and 1967, it was frowned upon to be a woman mathematician and he made it very difficult for me to continue my love for mathematics. He was known for a high failure rate and he did not like me questioning why my system was wrong…yet we both arrived at the same answer, just in different ways. Dr. Rothstein for Sociology was another professor I remember….Topics were very interesting, especially the theories dealing with television and the population persuasion/brainwashing. I enjoyed the demographic aspect of the course…

Dr. Burchard for science was phenomenal. Handsome with shiny dark hair and a great teacher….loved his classes.

Dr. Storch for Ancient Studies had an unusual sense of humor and the classes were good.

After UMBC:

- Taught in Anne Arundel County Publics Schools 1970-2006
- Elementary School Teacher, Special Education Teacher, Resource Teacher, Asst. Principal, Principal, and Supervisor, Human Resources
- Retired in 2006
- Now licensed as a Realtor
- Married Edward Doyle, class of August 1970, in November of 1970

- Lives in Catonsville, near son who graduated from UMBC Honors College and is currently the Deputy CIO and Senior Associate VP in the Division of Information Technology - UMBC
- Enjoys watching grandson grow and learning to drive as a sophomore in high school.
- Now serves on four Executive Boards for various organizations, Hospice volunteer, Legislative Committees

Dr. Janice Goldberg, Psychology, Teaching a Class

This Belongs to Mary Wyn Gillece Dudderar '70, American Studies

UMBC Jobs – Lessons Learned

My first work experiences were at UMBC. I started working on the PBX switchboard for Ceil. All calls coming into or going out of the University came through the switchboard. Ceil taught us the professional way to answer the phones and how to swiftly handle incoming calls. She urged us to provide quality customer service. In addition she was so kind and caring making us comfortable in sharing our concerns. Many of the lessons learned on this job helped me later in my work life when I trained new clerical staff.

My second job was in the Receiving Dept. All items coming into the university came through this Dept. Items received needed to be checked against Purchase Orders and then a receiving report was hand written to go to the business office. Once again my boss, Mr. Stozak stressed accuracy and good work habits. I interacted with the Business Office and answered phones regarding inquiries about reports and items received.

My third job was subbing for the Secretary to the Director of the Business Office. Mr. Brown was a kind man but he had an important job requiring efficient and quick response to questions. In this position I gained experience handling various inquiries, responding to them in a timely manner and with courtesy. I gained confidence and again good customer service qualities that became so important for my future work.

Working at UMBC in the early years made me feel valued, and work habits served me well in my future work life.

This Man was a Brilliant Teacher

Whenever I think of my time at UMBC I think of many special things, friends, jobs held and the great education I received. This education helped me become open to ideas even though they were different from mine. This education helped me to mature and to grow as an individual. There were many wonderful professors who helped me become an educated person but one professor stands out, Joel Jones. Although Dr. Jones wasn't at UMBC for very long his quality teaching, his ability to challenge his students and his belief in our potential helped us to be creative thoughtful students. He offered opportunities to visit his home and also encouraged us to attend a wonderful American Studies conference. This conference was enlightening regarding this major.

On a personal note, the summer my Father was gravely ill I took a summer class which was so helpful to keep my mind focused on an excellent course rather than on challenges in my life. When my father died Dr. Jones wrote me a beautiful sympathy note which meant so much to me. His caring words were thoughtful and offered such kind understanding. I continue to remember this man who was a brilliant teacher, someone who I admired whether on the basketball court or in the classroom. All the American Studies students were sad to see him leave. He went onto great things in his life as a leader in Higher Education.

After UMBC:

- Attended Graduate School at Virginia Commonwealth University in Rehabilitation Counseling
- Began work in 1970 at Springfield State Hospital as Industrial Therapist/Vocational Evaluator
- In 1973 worked for Maryland Department of Education, Division of Rehabilitation Services as a Rehabilitation Counselor in Frederick, then ended career as a Western Maryland Regional Director
- Married John Dudderar (attorney) in 1973
- Three Sons : Jason , CFA, First VP Morgan Stanley; Andrew, Electrician; Matthew, Major US Air Force, Pilot of U2
- 7 Grandchildren - 5 girls, 2 Boys

Dr. Joel Jones, American Studies

This Belongs to Steven K. Fedder '72, American Studies

Protests

April 29, 1970 – the US invades Cambodia. May 4, 1970 – the Ohio National Guard fires 67 live rounds in 13 seconds, killing 4 unarmed demonstrators at Kent State University. May 14, 1970 police open fire on a demonstration at Jackson State University, killing two. We Retrievers did not sit idly by. As protests mounted around the country, our campus was not immune. A student strike was called, and a group of us occupied Hillcrest – then the University's administration building. In what was likely the precursor to my professional career, I defended a fellow student in disciplinary proceedings, involving a claim by another student that the alleged miscreant had blocked her entrance to "Academic One" - then one of only two dedicated academic buildings on campus. The case was prosecuted by a university lawyer –who later became general counsel to the Johns Hopkins University. I was too stupid and naïve to believe that I could win the case, but as luck would have it, I did.

Those were heady times – not without reward. I made lifetime friends, fought to end the war in Vietnam, and even learned a few things. I have fond memories of classes with Paul Lauter, Jim Arnquist, Ed Orser, George Scheper, and Fred Pincus to name a few. The small campus and the youth of the faculty at the time made for close relationships between students and some of the faculty. Classes were often held in professors' homes, on the green, and at least once, on the Block to celebrate the 1970 Orioles World Series Victory.

A couple of events stand out. Once, during the protests against the war, we were having a teach-in outside on the lawn. College Park was at the time occupied by the National Guard. While all of this was going on, a contingent of National Guard troops saw the sign at Wilkens Avenue and the Beltway that simply said "University of Maryland." Thinking they had arrived at the College Park campus, the Guard arrived at our campus, observed that there was nothing much to see, and despite scaring us to death, went on their way. We were then but JV protesters I guess.

During that time we set up a "tent city" on the lawn, where some of us slept, but most of us being commuters, the tents were largely abandoned at night. Seizing what they saw as an opportunity to make their own statement, the UMBC lacrosse team took it upon themselves to knock down the encampment.

And we were not just concerned about the war. Some of the most popular professors on campus were denied tenure. We thought, and not without reason, that their activism led to the termination of their UMBC careers. This too became the subject of protest. The Academic Dean, one Homer Schamp, became the boogeyman. In a show of support, we had tee-shirts printed and distributed across campus with a picture of the Dean and the saying "Homer eats pie." So during a meeting in the theater classroom, in which Dr. Schamp was speaking, a still unidentified student hit him in the face with a shaving cream pie. Immediately afterward, the tee-shirts bloomed across campus. Of course, the University ignored our protests and did what it wanted.

To us now, these seem like childish pranks, and to some extent they were. But they were an important part of the college experience.

After UMBC:

- Trial lawyer for the last forty-five years.
- Chaired the Board of the Maryland Food Bank
- Chair of the Board of Trustees of the SEED School of Maryland, the only public boarding school in Maryland.
- Married with three children – the last of whom is a current UMBC student.
- "I'm proud to have graduated from a university that has done so much to prove that disadvantaged students, given the opportunity, can and do excel."

Protest at the Hillcrest Building, 1970

This Belongs to Louis C. Fiorucci, Jr. '71, Chemistry

Good Chemistry

I enrolled into the Chemistry/Science curriculum at UMBC in 1969, after graduating from a 4 year College Prep Program at The Baltimore City College (high school). As a kid, I received a Chemistry set (made by A. C. Gilbert, New Haven, Conn). From making chemical glues to flares, gun powder, and onward, I continued an interest in chemical science.

I entered UMBC in my Sophomore/Junior Years, and met Chemistry Department Chair Dr. Fred Gornick, Organic Professor Dr. Dale Whalen, Inorganic and Physical Chemistry Professors: Drs. Herb Silber, and Ellen Saegebarth. This faculty was very serious about the content of our studies and demanded a strong demonstration of understanding and completion of course materials. Since the University was still under development and construction, our classes met in either the Science or Library Building. Over time, there were more resources being made available.

I remember all three department classmates: Alan Martin, Fran Hughes, and Mike (from the 70's or early '71 class). Our small group met frequently to study, review lab work, clarify our understandings and prepare for exams. Being at UMBC was a challenging, rewarding, and enjoyable experience.

We never called out a bomb scare like some within the Organic Chemistry class did prior to their periodic exams.

Upon graduation, I felt that the Science (Physics/Biology, etc.) and Chemistry programs at UMBC provided me with a strong base for technical employment as well as future academic opportunities; and it did.

After UMBC:

- Graduated from UMCP 1974 BS/MS Chem. Engineering
- Worked as bench chemist
- Graduated from Johns Hopkins Public Health School 1990, MS Environmental Health Sciences
- Worked nationally and internationally for major inorganic chemical companies designing major facilities
- Married Christine Brooks, Now 51 years, one boy, one girl, 3 grandchildren
- Lives in New Windsor, Md. and retired in 2018 after 47 years

This Belongs to Joseph (Joe) Freed '70, English

Older than Some of the Dirt on the Campus

Just some thoughts about being part of the Founding Four:

For my freshman year, I wasn't at UMBC; I transferred in my sophomore year from College Park. Needless to say, UMBC was much smaller than the 45,000 students at College Park. It was a welcome change.

I remember the gym, the library's opening, the first lecture hall, the first dorms, Saturday nights listening to music and dancing at the coffee house. My psychology class was in the administration building on the hill. Getting towed out of my muddy parking space before there were so many parking lots, made my early finals session quite memorable.

For the most part, my professors were outstanding. Dr. Shedd (English) stands out as one of the most influential teachers in my life; he was a role model of the traits that make an outstanding teacher.

I took part in the campus social protests in 1970 and wore the white armband at graduation. The *Red Brick* newspaper was a truly unique feature of graduation, and the literary magazine during senior year raised such a furor over the beautiful photos of the dancers.

I was part of the first education class, and the outstanding new education professors "built the plane as we were flying it." But we finished our requirements (including a methods class on Saturday mornings), student taught, and applied for jobs for the following September.

UMBC's physical growth was amazing. While on sabbatical in 1982, I took courses at UMBC and never set foot on the part of the campus I had trod as an undergrad. In fact, when the old gym and multipurpose building were torn down, I realized I was, as the saying goes, "older than some of the dirt on the campus."

UMBC served me well. I am grateful for being one of the first to learn and to graduate from there. I have a sense of continual pride at being part of the first graduation class.

After UMBC:
- Served as English teacher and department chair for 22 years with Baltimore County Public Schools

- Served as part of the founding administrative staff (assistant principal and then principal) at George Washington Carver Center for Arts and Technology
- Retired from BCPS after 36 years
- Worked for the Maryland State Department of Education (MSDE) for 10 years as leadership development specialist
- Served as consultant and coach for the state's Promising Principals Academy
- Served as founding principal at the Baltimore Design School (Baltimore City Public Schools)
- Inducted into the Baltimore City College Alumni Hall of Fame in 2005
- Married in 1983, 3 children and 8 grandchildren
- Lives in Finksburg, Carroll County
- And worked part-time in the hospitality industry as an events bartender and restaurant host!

Always Under Construction

This Belongs to Sandra K. Geest '72, English

Older and Wiser

In 1967, we moved to Maryland for my husband's assignment to the Baltimore office of the Federal Highway Administration. I began college at Radford College (now Radford University) hoping to receive a degree in English and Library Science. I wanted to complete my degree and I actually applied to UMCP. I saw an article in The Baltimore Sun about a new campus near Baltimore that was a UM campus and decided to apply there, too, since it was closer to our new home in Ellicott City than College Park. My transcript was accepted at both places but I decided to attend UMBC to be closer to our son's school.

I was concerned that I was an older student compared to the students just out of high school. I needn't have been concerned because the other students showed no concern that I was older. Sometimes, I was even asked for advice about school, dating and my opinion on various things. One of the funniest memories is a MiniMester class that I took with Dr. Korenman, "Shakespeare's Theatre" where I had to bring my 5 year old son to class with me. The public school was closed for the Christmas Holiday and I did not have a baby sitter. I asked Dr. Korenman if I could bring him to class with me if we sat in the back of the class, he was quiet and if he wasn't, we would leave class. She said, fine with her. We got to class early, sat in the back and he had his drawing paper and crayons and was instructed to be very quiet and if he was, we would get an ice cream cone on the way home. Students started to come into the class, a couple of girls sat in front of us. I overheard their conversation. "Wow, do you see that kid behind us? They are letting people in here at UMBC younger and younger." I got a real laugh out of that remark.

When the public school opened, the first day my son's teacher had "Show and Tell" time for her class where the students told what they had done on vacation. When she got to my son, he said, "I went to UMBC to college to Shakespeare class and I learned all about The Globe Theatre." The teacher called me and asked if he was making a story up for her class. I told her that what he told her was true. She and I were really surprised that he was paying attention and accurately described The Globe Theatre complete with a drawing that he did. I thought that he was just doodling the whole time and instead Dr. Korenman had taught a 5 year old quite a bit about Shakespeare and the Theatre. I often wondered if the other college students in the class learned as much as my 5 year old son, Steven.

After UMBC:

- Employed as District Sales Manager for Fortune 500 Company for 10 years-1970-1980
- Employed by James W. Rouse, Columbia, MD, as Conference and Special Events Planner. Managed VIP events including events at White House Rose Garden, House and Senate Office bldg. and National Building Museum, 1980-1998.
- Retired in 1998 and moved to beach home on the Chesapeake Bay in Calvert County, MD.
- Served as President of UMBC Alumni Association twice, 1st woman President.
- Represented UMBC and first president of UM Alumni Association International
- President twice, served on Board of Directors and Chancellor's Advisory Council
- Awarded UMBC Volunteer of the Year 1990.
- Married to James G. Geest (Jay), one son, Steven
- President and Secretary of Citizen's Association
- Sings with Encore Creativity, a national Chorale group for adults over 50.
- Performed at The Kennedy Center, on the Queen Mary, at Westminster Abbey Cathedral and other cathedrals in London, England. Singing at Strathmore in 2022.

Lecture Hall One

The Belongs to Abraham Gertner '70, History

Reflections

Story #1: First day at UMBC: I can remember when we are all gathered outside of the lecture hall as we talked to those of us we knew from City College. We went here because it was cheap, cheaper than Baltimore Community College (now known as BCCC) and smaller than it. We started a political science group and even had speakers come to UMBC. One was Clarence Mitchell III from the state legislature. Professor Frank Burd was our sponsor and he said trying to bring famous speakers to UMBC was like asking them to come to the desert.

Story #2: One of the most important things for our first year or two was CARPOOLING… We would sit in the cafeteria waiting for our riders and or driver. Most of us had families with only one car. There were several days each week that I thumbed my way (hitchhiked) to downtown where I worked as a law clerk after classes. On the days I drove carpool, I would take my father to work first downtown and then come back towards UMBC….a very early start to the day. Remember: we were commuters…there were no dorms.

Story #3: I remember some of the phenomenal student activities to help bring culture to UMBC. A concert pianist performed, Otis Redding came and we did pay $5 for that special event. Very often we stayed on Friday or came back Saturday for movies in the lecture hall.

After UMBC:

- Worked as Juvenile Counselor 1970-1974
- Studied and became attorney in 1974
- Still practicing law now
- Lives in Ellicott City, MD
- Living nearby are 2 adult children and 3 grandchildren

Registering for Classes

This Belongs to Rob Goald '70, Biological Sciences

Rockin' the Campus

From 1966 to 1970, I researched performing and recording artists who represented a wide range of musical genres. I was part of a committee authorized by the UMBC Administration to seek out and book talent from among the plethora of groups from all over the world. Faculty Member Phil Landon was committee chairman and I was one of two students invited to be on the committee.

The first act to perform on the UMBC campus was folk rock singer, song writer and guitarist Tim Buckley. Buckley performed his signature song, "Buzzin' Fly" as a warm up before his first set. He was born in Washington DC, but was bringing his psychedelic, jazz fusion, blue-eyed soul musical style from Los Angeles. I picked Buckley up from BWI airport, known back then as Friendship Airport, getting him to the campus for his performance. We lost him in 1975 to a heroin and morphine overdose at the age of 28.

Continuing to attract rock groups gaining popularity in the mid to late '60s, I invited Earth Opera, an American psychedelic rock group founded by Peter Rowan and David Grisman. The band did a mix of folk and psychedelic rock. I was disappointed that they omitted one of their songs "Death by Fire". They did, however, offer "The Red Sox are Winning", an anti-war protest song which attempted to show the American preoccupation with sports, while the war raged on in Southeast Asia.

Later, I tried to get up close and personal with the Incredible String Band performing on campus. They were a psychedelic folk band which formed in Edinburgh in 1966 and were considered pioneers in that field of music. I marched into their private trailer and used their bathroom facilities during one of their performances. They really got "pissed off" at me!

When Chicago Transit Authority, later just Chicago, landed on campus in 1967-68, they became upset at the low turnout for a performance and decided to do one set for 45 minutes instead of the originally planned two sets. Attendance was low because nobody knew who they were.

Music performers were not the only ones I ferried from the airport to campus, however. I once transported Abbie Hoffman to the Johns Hopkins sponsored Hippie House located at that time at Reisterstown Road and Naylors Lane off of Old Court Road. It was a favorite hangout for a number of performers and celebrities of that time. Lou Reed of Velvet Underground stayed there before their UMBC performance. It has been torn down since, following a raid by the Baltimore County Police Department. Guests were greeted there by Velvet Chief who provided special refreshments of the day. Doug Wankin was the house director. I took some members of the UMBC administration to meet with Abbie Hoffman at Hippie House.

Later, I accompanied Abbie Hoffman to a Speakers Movement Bureau on Manhattan's Lower East Side. David Peel, a local musician and army veteran, joined with Hoffman at the time of protests against the Vietnam War and in support of the push for legalizing marijuana. Musicians and politicians came together with Abbie Hoffman.

Another celebrity I brought on campus to speak was Paul Krassner, the editor of Realist Magazine. It was a satirical underground publication of articles and some interviews and political commentary from protest voices of the day.

Velvet Underground and Fallen Angels were on the bill at one campus performance. I had an $1100 check for Lou Reed of Velvet Underground who did it all for that group including writing most of their songs. Lou almost lost that check while we were out at the Hippie House! I took Lou to my home for a stay while in town too.

Other Velvet Underground band members were Sterling Morrison with a Ph.D, Doug Yule, and a female drummer named Maureen Tucker. Andy Warhol sponsored Velvet Underground. Captain Beefheart, another experimental rock artist of the day, used to say that he didn't pay for the music he was playing and that we shouldn't pay for it either. Sometimes we did though. We also tried to book Linda Ronstadt for a concert but we just could not cut a deal, but we were able to book the Fifth Avenue Band. That was my last major act booked as a member of the UMBC committee.

I was also an admirer of Jack Walsh, the editor of the UMBC campus Red Brick newspaper, circulated alongside the standard campus newspaper, The Retriever. Before that, Jack was editor of the City Paper in Baltimore. He had a 4.0 average in American Studies, and he was a good friend of local playwright John Waters. Waters gave Walsh a part in "Pink Flamingo" and borrowed a bunch of money from Jack which Waters never paid back. Jack Walsh died in poverty.

While we were at UMBC, Poet and writer Alan Ginsberg came to speak at Goucher College but not at UMBC. I interviewed him anyway and loaned out the recording of the interview to someone at Hippie House but never got it back.

UMBC is mentioned in the Trial of the Chicago 7 movie where seven defendants are charged by the federal government with conspiracy in connection with the protests at the 1968 Democratic National Convention.

After UMBC:

- Over 30 years-experience as journalist, author, filmmaker, broadcast studio specialist, radio producer, educator
- Freelance journalist for Journal of Film and Video, The Baltimore Sun, Baltimore City Paper, In-Motion Magazine, Markee Magazine, Sculpture Magazine
- Senior Editor at Film Festival Today from 2004-2020
- Full time faculty member at University of Nevada Las Vegas from 2004- 2020
- Former full time faculty member at Baltimore City College, American University, Fitchburg State College, DeSales University, adjunct professor at UMBC, Towson State University
- Inducted into the Las Vegas Film Critics Society in 2010
- Book in progress on the best independent films ever made across the globe
- Stepped down from professor position at UNLV and editor position at Film Festival in 2020 due to onset of Parkinson's Disease

TIM BUCKLEY AND EARTH OPERA
U. M. B. C. · 5401 WILKENS AVENUE
SATURDAY, NOVEMBER 9, 1968 at 8:30 P. M.
$1.50 FOR STUDENTS WITH I. D. $3.00 FOR VISITORS

This Belongs to Arnold (Arnie) Golberg '73, American Studies

The Dorms Open

I arrived at UMBC in 1968. We went to Hillcrest to register for classes. Hillcrest was an old house* and the classes that were still open were on a big chalk board. As each class filled the classes were erased. We sat on the floor and selected classes. Most closed quickly because of the class size. The registrar was Judith Hirsch; she helped navigate incoming freshman. I commuted the first year and in 1969 the dorms opened and I was one of the first to move in. I recall there were about 250 of us in our new home. There was a husband and wife director team. Arthur Libby I think was the "head man". We called him Uncle Arthur (behind his back of course.) Hey we were kids. It was called dorm one. Later we thought we would call it Robert Hall a local clothier or Hee Haw a television program. Smarter people vetoed those names. The men were on the basement floor. I was in room 023. It was a suite, i.e. 2 rooms separated by a bathroom with a shower. Each room had a sink with a bed and stand-alone closet. Each had a telephone with our own private number. The opposite side of the hall had study classes. The main floor with the lobby was occupied by the women and the third and top floor alternating men and women. Each floor had a rec room where we could prepare some meals as the dining hall had not been completed. Each floor also had a resident assistant. We ate at Paul's restaurant in Arbutus, Howard Johnson's on Rt. 40 for all you can eat fried chicken. (They hated when 10 of the men walked in) and Father's Gay 90's on Frederick Rd. There was a Student Union, the cafeteria, Lecture Hall One and the library. To get to the library we had to walk on wooden boards as the pavement had not been completed. We pretty much self-governed ourselves and we had student officers and each floor had a president. We would live in our new home, albeit we had "battles' with the directors. We worked them out as I recall. We even had a parents visiting day when we broke into small groups and the parents saw how we lived and we had lunch in the dining hall.

The classes as mentioned were small; I think 40 or so except Lecture Hall One where there may have been 100 or more students. In the classrooms one could eat and even smoke with hard aluminum ash trays provided. Attendance was rarely taken. I re-call a freshman asking a professor if attendance is taken and he said, "It's your nickel, spend it any way you want." I had many great teachers. Dr. Nancy Henly; Dr. Burd, Dr. Orser, a favorite and many more.

I received a fine education at UMBC. I still have my ID card!! 4 years at UMBC was the best time of my life other than marrying my high school sweetie.

My great nephew was just accepted and will be living on campus. From generation to generation.

> *Hillcrest was actually part of the Spring Grove State Hospital facilities, as was the land upon which UMBC was constructed. Specifically, Hillcrest housed the criminally insane.

After UMBC:

- Began career as a part time teacher in the city schools and went to graduate school for 3 years.
- After nine years working for a local company, bought Clothworks, a commercial and residential re-upholstery company that employed up to 23 people in a commercial setting in Baltimore.
- Now semi-retired and working from home.
- Married 50 years in January 2023 (unless Dorathy comes to her senses)
- Two granddaughters and two grandsons.
- "At UMBC the most important message was that I was taught to think. Life is good: Just like I planned."

Dorm One Under Construction

This Belongs to Dale Gough '70, American Studies

Before There was UMBC

I grew up on Poplar Ave in Arbutus, just down the street from the property that would become the campus. In 1964 we began to see activity taking place on what had been the farm that had been part of Spring Grove State Hospital. By late 1964 and early 1965 construction crews were beginning to erect buildings just out of sight from what was at the time Walker Ave. Each day my school bus traveled that road on the way to take me to Catonsville High School.

The Man on a Tractor

It was the summer of 1966. I had graduated from Catonsville High and was planning on three months of sleep and nothingness. Mrs. Gough had other ideas. She had seen an ad in the Arbutus Times that the school under construction at the end of my street (Poplar Ave) was hiring ground crew for the summer. It became clear that my summer plans were going to change.

So, one Saturday in early June I found myself outside of the 'old gray house' on the hill (then close to the current location of the Event Center) with several others eager to meet with Mr. Chisolm, the Director of the Physical Plant, about working on the crew.

When we arrived at the appointed hour there was a man riding a tractor cutting grass around the gray house. Another man was in the house on the phone. We could hear him speaking through the screen. Finally, as the phone call ended one of us opened the screen door and said, "Dr. Kuhn, we're here to meet with Mr. Chisolm about the ground crew jobs. The reply? "I'm Guy Chisolm. Dr. Kuhn is on the tractor. I'll be with you in just a minute."

Whoa...the president is cutting grass on a tractor, while the guy in charge of getting the grass cut is sitting in the 'office' on the phone? What kind of alternative universe had I fallen into? I got the job and worked on the grounds for two summers. (I should point out that the grounds crew were paid $1.35 an hour, while those working inside were paid $1.25.)

That evening at the dinner table I announced I had decided to attend this new school (still under construction) rather than Towson State College (I had been admitted to both). Mrs. Gough cried thinking that a school that had been around for almost 100 years was a better choice than one not even open. Later that night as my Dad was heading to bed, he stuck his head in my bedroom. "You made the right choice, the better choice today. Any man willing to do the least of jobs in their organization is a really good person and his example should be followed."

I've never regretted that decision. In the past year, I've wondered what my life would have been had UMBC not been built across from my street. Probably I would have gone to Towson but getting there would have been a challenge. My parents didn't have enough money for room and board, and not enough for a third car. That would have meant the bus with a transfer downtown and an hour and a half travel time each way. A friend on the next street went to Towson - but he was transferring to UMBC.

I hope I have followed the example of that man on a tractor cutting grass.

Things I Never Told my Parents

When I enrolled in 1966 I signed up for a Baltimore County tuition assistance program whereby I agreed to teach in the County after graduation for a reduced tuition. By the end of my first year I was knocking on the door of academic probation. I missed the part of the program that required a GPA higher than mine.

I didn't want my parents to know how poorly I had done, so when tuition was due for the Fall 1967 I asked for a check in the same amount as for the previous year. Crisis averted, but not eliminated.

I had worked on the grounds crew in the summer of 1966 and 1967 and in the Biology labs during the academic year 1966-67, but realized I needed more hours to make ends meet. I realized that the Library was open seven days a week and well into the evenings. So I switched to the library. Theoretically, student workers were only to work 20 hours a week, but thankfully, the professional staff allowed me to get in 30 hours or more.

I thought my secret was about to be revealed when around the time of our 1970 graduation my Dad asked 'what about teaching'? (By that time, I had enlisted in the Army – as my draft lottery number was low.) Quickly thinking, I told him that because I was going into the service, the obligation to teach was waived.

Teaching in MiniMester

As a result of a paper I had done as an American Studies Special Project course in the fall of 1968, Dr. Joel Jones asked if I was interested in teaching a course on Native American History during the January 1969 MiniMester. Of course I would! He then said I would co-teach with Betty Huesman, who had also done a paper on Native American Culture.

My portion covered the history of the Cherokee Nation, especially concerning the Cherokee newspaper which was one of the first printed newspapers in America. Betty's emphasis spoke to the cultural aspects of the various Native Nations.

We were paid – I think $400 – and we were the first undergraduates to teach a credit-bearing course in Maryland. Dean Homer Schamp had to 'go to bat' for us as the folks in Annapolis had never had such a request before.

After UMBC:

- Married Gail Buffington (former UMBC student), 1969. Two children, Joel (Deceased 2012) and Megan. Megan and husband, Ken (also a UMBC graduate) live in Hampstead MD with their two children, Kenny (UMBC Class of 2030) and Lauren (UMBC Class of 2033).
- Enlisted US Army (Military Intelligence), served in Panama, 1971-73. Nominated for the White House Fellows Program by the US Southern Command
- Master of Arts in Human Relations, University of Oklahoma (Canal Zone) 1974.
- Directed International Admissions, University of Maryland, College Park, 1974-1991. Received a Fulbright Administrators grant to Germany, 1982
- Director, International Education Services, American Association of Collegiate Registrars and Admissions Officers (AACRAO), 1992-2016.
- Authored or edited 30+ publications on international educational systems. Made presentations on U.S. education in Canada, Mexico, United Kingdom, Germany, the Czech Republic, Panama, Costa Rica, Guatemala, Taiwan, China, and Japan.
- Served on the College Board International Advisory Council. Served on the TOEFL (Test of English as a Foreign Language) Advisory Council.
- Serves on the McCormick Scholarship Selection Committee (International and Domestic)
- Director, Foreign Credentials Service of America (2016-present).
- Lives in Catonsville.

UMBC Campus Under Construction, 1965

This Belongs to Donna Banks Hekler '70, English

A Charcuterie of Memories

Acceptance
I was accepted to UMBC in the winter of my high school Junior year on just my grades. I took the SAT and ACT and submitted the grades, but I already had my acceptance letter.

It's New
Starting a new school is like being thrown into the ocean, naked. You had to keep your head above water, be creative and paddle hard. We didn't follow traditions; we created them.

"Louie" Sowers wanted women's volleyball (and women's sports in general), so she created a team. Not only was no authority on that new campus planning on women playing intercollegiate sports, they were shocked women wanted it. Ted Raitch taught karate; a skill he had learned during his military service in Vietnam.

Other students created:
> The Retriever, newspaper
> Skipjack, yearbook
> The Red Brick, alternative newspaper
> The Senior Project, which donated scholarship funds
> Proms

Some of the things we started have endured; some have not. What premise does endure is that we created the mold, the platform; the foundation on which the school rests.

Rides
In the first years getting to UMBC was not easy. The Baltimore transit system ran near the campus, but the route was an alternative, so the buses were sparse at best. If you missed the bus, it could be hours before another one came. Also it was a good 30 minute walk to the bus stop.

Therefore, people who did not have cars tried to find rides. I spent many hours in the cafeteria or at the "study carrels" in the Biology building. We would leave notes on the bulletin board for who wanted and who would give rides. That is how I met Bonnie Hurwitz and Aldona Drazdys.

In my junior year, I got a car. Freedom at last.

Cafeteria

It's not often a building takes on the personality of a person, but the 1966 cafeteria certainly did. In the first years, we had three buildings; lecture hall, classroom/professors' offices/library and the cafeteria/gym. The cafeteria became the hub, the center of campus life. It was the only place to get food or a drink, other than water fountains. Everyone ate there, students, faculty, and staff. It was usual for these three groups to mix and share tables together. There was no us and them; we were all just one big family, experimenting in birthing something new. Ideas were exchanged, some radical, opinions expressed, friendships made.

It was really the only place to go on campus. In order to be an accredited university, you had to have a library and a gym. To meet the library requirement, a "library" was created in a classroom, until the permanent structure was built. It was small, limited and not very useful. This is coming from someone who went to The Enoch Pratt Library in Baltimore on a regular basis, especially since one of my bus stops to get home was right in front. We knew the day was coming for a beautiful library, but maybe after we graduated. So to the cafeteria we went.

And it was in the cafeteria we stayed. If you wanted to find someone, just sit in the cafeteria, they would show up. Since the cafeteria was close to the ONE parking lot, after leaving your car, a stroll thru the space to check the vibe of day, catch up on any news or see if someone was looking for you was de rigueur. At the end of the day, same path, only in reverse.

I tried to convince myself it was a place to study while waiting for rides, but the temptation to socialize always won out over books. If nothing else, you could go watch the rotating pitch game that was never ending. As one person left for class, someone always filled in one of the four seats. I knew the game as my family played it, but I never joined in. The regulars verged on professional and I was not that good. It was fun to be a fly on the wall.

I met my best friend Rene there, which led to meeting my first husband. And of course, there was the infamous lunch with Crazy Maria.

Trilogy – Lunch

The cafeteria was packed and there I stood with my cafeteria tray. There's Maria (Adams Raitch) with a distinguished looking well-dressed man and two open seats – score. After walking over and asking her if I could join them, she said sure. Maria was an American Studies major and I was English, so it was accepted for us to have different professors. Also seeing professors eating with students was an everyday occurrence. The cafeteria was the only place on campus that served food; not even a snack vending machine. That was just the campus we built. There were no Ivory Towers; educators were respected but not holy and put on pedestals. Dialogue happened everywhere and where better than over a meal? Another normality was that something crazy always happens around Maria. That's why her nickname was Crazy Maria.

I sat down and after a few minutes her professor said "Maria, I don't know this young lady, why don't you introduce me?" Maria said "Sure, Donna please meet Dr. Kuhn!"

DR. KUHN, The Chancellor, The God, The Big Kahuna HERE, at this cafeteria table, with me. Oh My God have I been minding my manners; am I buttoned and zipped; do I have food in my teeth? Crazy Maria strikes again.

Once I recovered from the shock, Dr. Kuhn engaged us in conversation. He wanted to know what was working, and more importantly, what was not. No sugar coated answer here please. He encouraged us to be thoughtful and honest. We complied.

This was a transformational experience for me. It was the first time an adult, much less one of this stature, had ever encouraged, listened to and valued my opinion.

Trilogy – The Chat
I was walking to class one day in my Junior year and coming the other way was Dr. Kuhn. As UMBC grew and duties piled on, we saw less and less of him on campus. I was so excited so see him, as I truly loved and revered the man. I spoke to him saying "Dr. Kuhn, it's so good to see you on campus; we never see you here anymore." He stopped and we chatted for a brief moment and then he walked on. Then I noticed the 10 distinguished men following him.

Trilogy - The Reunion
Dr. Kuhn came to a reunion; I think the 25th. By then he was in a wheelchair as his health had deteriorated and he was nearly blind. After the program, I went over to him, knelt down, took his hand and said, "Dr. Kuhn, it's so good to see you. It's Donna Banks." He lifted his head to look in my direction and said, "Donna, it's good to see you too. I recognize your voice."

No Football or Greek Social Life
To understand why there is no football, or social fraternities or sororities at UMBC you need to understand the social times in which the school started and it would help if you have seen the Movie "Animal House".

It's the mid-1960s, social justice was just starting, the war in Vietnam was raging, The Black Panthers were speaking out for black rights, the SDS (Students for a Democratic Society) and more radical Weathermen, were protesting the war. John Kennedy, Bobby Kennedy and Martin Luther King had been assassinated. Parents did not understand why their children were marching and protesting; shouldn't they be just doing what their parents told them to do? Wasn't this how the world was supposed to be, obedient children, just like they had been?

We pushed the boundaries on clothing wearing, bell bottom and hip hugger pants, midriff baring tops known as crop tops, very short skirts i.e., miniskirts (a few of which were seen at UMBC) and bikinis. Our parents were appalled.

Girls were still living under the old model of going to college to learn to be nurses and teachers and find a husband. There were few to no opportunities for women in business. I applied to a large utility company and was told that even with a college degree that everyone started their career at the company by climbing poles. Sorry I did not complete a degree to work on an outside line crew in winter with no clear path of progression in the company.

Some guys were in college just to avoid the draft and being sent to Vietnam. The draft dodgers, as they were known, attended just enough classes to stay in school.

We saw friends go to schools where their major was party. Football games with tailgate parties were the highlight of the school week. Guys joined fraternities for the never ending revelry and to get away from restrictive dorm life. Also in order to join a fraternity you had to "pledge" and go through Hell Week; a week of doing stupid things designed to humiliate you. This activity is supposed to create a bond between brothers. I personally saw it as demeaning and dangerous. We heard reports of students who died, often from being forced to drink too much alcohol.

Football also created a syndrome known as the Big Man on Campus (BMOC). The BMOC was usually the football team's quarterback. Women wanted to be with him; Men wanted to be him. This accolade had nothing to do with academics and in my opinion was divisive. One or two people were honored more than others. We wanted none of that. We wanted inclusion, a chance for everyone. All you had to do was work and be the best you, you could be. Everyone had the same chance to succeed.

So we stood against groups or activities that excluded or had the potential to hurt people. We wanted UMBC to be known for fairness, academics, inclusion and achievement.

A Plethora of Professors
Dr. Jones
I was in the cafeteria getting ready to go to class. This was the first day of class and we were just beginning to meet our professors. When someone asked about my class, I replied English 101 with Joel Jones. One of the women sitting at the table said "Oh My God – he is gorgeous".

I was in English 101 with Joel Jones. One of the students, Glenn, announced his intention to become a writer. He revealed that he wrote when he became *"inspired"*. Dr. Jones immediately retorted that professional writers got up in the morning, went to their office and wrote for 8 hours. It is a job, a profession, a discipline and inspiration is not the motivation.

Dr. Lewis
In the first semester of my freshman year, Dr. Lewis offered his course on Population. This was appealing, as I was very interested in the subject; he was on the President's Council after the census; he had written the textbook. It was exciting to me to learn from someone with this pedigree. Unfortunately, I felt I could not enroll, as I had to focus on taking required courses, not electives, as my Maryland State Teacher Scholarship was only good for 4 years. Also he did not offer the course every semester.

When I was a Junior, Dr. Lewis offered the course again. YEAH! I went to my advisor, Dr. Mahaney, and pleaded my case. He said it was unusual for a Junior to be taking a freshman level course, but he understood the circumstances and signed off on my request.

Later I was in the English suite of offices and one of the other professors stopped me and said that he noticed I was taking a freshman level course, which he found highly irregular. He said he never would have approved it if I were his advisee. I replied, "Yes and that is why you are not my advisor".

Dr. Mahaney
All English majors were required to take a semester course in Shakespeare taught by Dr. William Mahaney. This was a Junior level course, so we all were all familiar with writing papers and therefore, the standard editing comments. Dr. Mahaney returned our first papers and proceeded to fill the boards with said editing comments. Most papers had as much red on them as black. There was unfortunately one comment no one knew. Someone had the courage to raise their hand and inquire about the new designation to the papers, "OCN" Dr. Mahaney's response "Oh Come Now".

Dr. Low
I was in History 101 with Dr. Low. It was 2 or 3pm MWF. Before the class on the first Friday of May, a few of us asked Dr. Low if he would consider cancelling class, as it was Flower Mart.

We explained that going to Flower Mart was long established Baltimore tradition for many of us and something we had been doing since childhood. In 1964 that was how I celebrated my 16th birthday. (I even remember the dress I made to wear for this special occasion.) If he cancelled, many of us could keep our Baltimore tradition.

He refused. We were crestfallen. The responsibilities of adulthood were looming large. He also said there would be large repercussions if any of us cut class and that he would take role to ensure our attendance. Unhappy but compliant, we came.

He took roll and said "Students I will see you Monday and walked out."
He cancelled class; but then it was too late in the day to go.

I still haven't forgiven him.

Dr. Alice Robinson
Freshman year I took Speech 101 with Dr. Alice Robinson, head of the department. She was a stately, proper woman, with piercing blue eyes and because she was from Kansas, had no accent.

The class met 3 times a week and 3 people would speak at each meeting. In the last round of speeches, I was up. When I finished, Dr. Robinson told me to see her in her office. I went.

Her comment was that my speech was very good, and if I kept up that level of work, I would most likely receive an A. She also said, however, if you don't get rid of the B'more accent, you will surely fail. My comment - What accent. She just shook her head and said "you have a lot of work to do, and you just lost 2 and a half weeks of the class". (PS: I got my A and went on to do enough classes to accomplish 15 credits in the discipline.)

Dr. Bettridge
All English majors were required to take a Linguistics class and Dr. Bettridge was the only professor who taught it. Trapped. He was tough, so most people avoided his classes, if at all possible. No such luck here. A major part of our grade was to phonetically transcribe a document on which we had no practice. Scary.

When I got my paper back, I had gotten a B-, yeah, but the grade was knocked down to C+. What – how did that happen? So, off to discuss it with The Devil (gulp). Dr. Bettridge said I lost the points because of the heading, which consisted of name (Donna Banks), date, and class name and number. This was really confusing to me; I mean the heading was part of the paper? And what could I have done wrong on the heading?

Simple, I had transcribed my last name incorrectly. What? There is a symbol in phonetics that represents an NG sound and I had used it in my last name, so my name came out, Bangs (not Banks). I said Dr. Bettridge, that's how I say my name. He said no: I said yes. He said "Say your name"; I did – Bangs. He said yes that is how YOU say your name, but that is not how your name is said. Your problem is not that you can't hear, it's that you can't speak. The C- remained. (PS remember the Baltimore accent with Dr. Robinson.)

Dr. Roswell
To complete my language requirement, I took 2 semesters of French with Dr. Roswell. She made me a deal at the end of my second semester. I would get a C if I never, ever, ever spoke French again. It's been 53 years and I've kept my part of the bargain.

Dr. Brown....History of Music
I took this class as one of my electives. For the final exam Marion Brown was going to play a short clip of music and we had to identify the piece. This was in the days of record players so it meant dropping the needle in just the right spot. We were very concerned about getting this right, as it was an important part of our grade. Then we heard the four notes da, da, da, da one of the most recognizable pieces of music ever. She meant to drop it just a tad further in. Reprieved.
I was a member of the choir and we did a concert, mainly of madrigals and medieval music. I was a first soprano and had to come in on an A over high C. With the help of Marion Brown, I hit the note. Was very proud of myself.

Dr. Shedd – final course
English majors were required to take a final course with Dr. Shedd, head of the department, in order to graduate. We were all apprehensive about this course, as it was made very clear, that if we failed, we would not graduate. (A disaster for me, as I was on a scholarship and had to get out in four years.)

The first night of class Shedd handed out the "reading list"; poems, plays, novels, short stories, everything. This is what we were **supposed** to have read in the four years at UMBC. It was thirty pages long! Everyone was in shock to see how little they had accomplished. Then Dr. Shedd had us make a list of everything we had not read. I was so embarrassed about how unaccomplished I felt, that I started leaving things out. Some people were more honest than me and wrote down everything, as we were sure Dr. Shedd would go through the list and make a composite class reading list. Dummies. He collected the lists, handed out the class syllabus and class reading list. The list was ALL CRITICAL WORKS; not one piece from the dreaded reading list.

The next announcement was he would review the lists he had just collected, make a personal additional reading list for each of us and review them in our required personal meetings. We were doomed.

For our final English class, we had class and personal meetings with Dr. Shedd, head of the department. He also held our fate in his hands, as we had to pass his class to graduate. In a personal meeting with him I asked why Paradise Lost was on the reading list. What I really wanted to know is how do you evaluate "A Classic"; why has one work become a classic and to endure time and another not. What makes Moby Dick (which I despise) so enduring? Dr. Shedd looked at me and said "You are impossible. The written word is lost on you. I need to start with pictures" and proceeded to open Art History works from his shelves. (PS I passed the class.)

Birthday party personifies relationships
In his office, we threw Dr. Mahaney a birthday party, complete with goofy paper hats. The relationship between students and faculty at UMBC was different than most colleges. Most colleges in that era had students regarding their professors as gods on high. They were revered as fonts of knowledge and lowly students should be grateful for any gems that came their way. Not so at UMBC. It was a collaboration, rather than a servitude.

We heard stories of students at other schools being in lecture halls of 500 people taught by a graduate student, not a professor. Individual meetings also were with the said graduate students. Many students in other schools did not encounter Doctorate level instructors until they were Juniors. We had none of that. Ninety-five percent of my classes were taught by educators with full doctorates. Their command of the subject was impeccable, because their doctorate was in the subject they were teaching. Often the teacher had written the textbook. This encouraged us to work harder and to keep up. We were held to a higher standard, everywhere.

In most schools, research assistant positions and people who worked for professors went to upperclassmen and graduate students. As we had neither of these, opportunities came to us that most underclassmen would never see. This holds true today. Underclassmen were not fodder to be forgotten but encouraged to innovate.

We were taught by these mentors; some of whom were just a few years older than us. We also played sports with them. Went on MiniMester trips with them. Debated and listened to them. Shared meals at restaurants. And we threw them birthday parties, with water guns filled with more than water. Having these relationships were a treasure and most unusual.

Friendship and Fun
Rene
I met my friend Rene in the cafeteria. She had just transferred in from Salisbury and was in my English class, so I said lets go to class together. Rene got married and had a child before we graduated. When her daughter got old enough, Rene came back to school. I had a class at 9am and she had a class at 10am in the same room. Halfway through the semester, her babysitter quit. I suggested she bring Sandy to class and I would sit her for the hour class, but with one condition; Sandy had to wear a harness.

Sandy was just learning to walk and she spent her time falling down or letting go of your hand and running away. This scared me, as I was sure she was going to bolt just as a class let out and disaster would ensue. I pictured 100 students barreling out of class totally oblivious to the small unstable person in my care. The study desks were close by and the sharp corners were eye height to a 2 year old. The harness gave her freedom and me piece of mind.

While babysitting Sandy, my friend's daughter in the classroom building 3 times a week for a half semester, I had to find a creative way to keep a 2 year old occupied. She LOVED riding in the elevator. As I held her in my arms, someone would come on and Sandy would gleefully push the floor button. It was a great game and Sandy learned her numbers.

Shirley
Shirley Coursey was an English major who was in her forties (or maybe older). After raising her children, she decided to come to UMBC to finish her English degree. She graduated Summa Cum Laude, and may have had the best GPA of our class.

The Retriever decided to interview her because the staff was sure students would want to hear what someone of her accomplishment was going to do after graduation. Ideals ran high in those early years and many people were on a MISSION to Save the World, or at least Make Their Mark. Shirley agreed to the interview and the question the reporter asked her was "What are you going to DO when you graduate?" Shirley's response "I'm going to paint my basement". The reporter was flabbergasted, and appalled. He wanted to know her purpose; what was she going to accomplish; how was she going to contribute to society. So, he asked the same question again. Shirley's response was the same. The reporter left befuddled with head spinning. I am sure Shirley picked a nice color.

Henry
Just before graduation, I bought Henry Roberts' bike. He needed the money for his plane ticket to go to his Peace Corps assignment.

Etchings
One of my friends was invited by a professor to see his etchings. When she found said etchings were in his bedroom, she politely declined, as she was concerned he might be interested in showing her more than just his etchings.

Dance Decorations
I was on the organizing committee for one of the dances. We wanted decorations, but funds were very limited. At the time, I was working in the computer department of Hutzler's Brothers Department store. Every day we threw away stacks of blue, orange and pink punch cards. I brought them to campus and we stapled them together to make streamers. Very colorful.

The Dorm
In the second semester of our Senior year, the Dorm opened. I applied to move in and be a proctor, as proctors received compensation. With the compensation, I could make it work. Finally time to move out of my parents' house.

Unfortunately, I was not accepted. The "authorities" wanted Juniors, as they would stay for 3 semesters, not my one. Another strike against me was my last semester would be consumed with student teaching and they felt teaching would interfere with my duties as a proctor. Staying in my bedroom on Wilkens Avenue.

The Literary Magazine
I took a copy home. The cover was a black and white picture of modern dancers, nude. My father went nuts and wanted to know what we were being taught and threatened to pull me out of school.

The Hole
The Kuhn family lived on campus at the top of the hill overlooking what is now the library. The start of the library building was to dig a deep hole for the foundation, right behind the Kuhn home. One day one of the children drove the

family car and forgot to set the parking brake. The car wound up front bumper first in the hole. The campus was a twitter over that one.

Typing
Legend was, typewritten papers got a half to a full grade higher than hand written. I had taken typing in high school in preparation for college, but I was not very good. In fact, it was the only class in high school where I received a D. The grade would have been an F, but I was college prep and typing was an elective, hence I could not fail.

I only had a manual typewriter and my fingers did not have equal strike strength, so some letters were darker than others. Because I made mistakes, there were erasures and retyping of letters. In short, a mess. I was an English major, so there were lots of papers.

Finally one of my professors suggested I hand write my papers. I complied.

Stop the World I Want to Get Off
Was a popular play in the era, and the Theatre Department decided to produce it. I had been in the choir, so I knew I could deliver the musical part. I was so excited to try out and really, really, really wanted to be selected. I GOT THE PART. Yeah. Then I got the rehearsal schedule. Oh My God. There was no way I could meet the time requirement of the rehearsal schedule and do all the semester reading for my English major. I gave up my part. Now I know why my theatre friends never came to class and were always borrowing my notes.

The Finale
Helen
With her two canes and misshapen legs, Helen Hopkins was one of the most visibly recognizable people on campus. Walking, a simple skill we all took for granted, was a heroic effort for Helen, as she had Cerebral Palsy as a child.

More amazing than her determination to get to class was her spirit. She continuously had a smile on her face. She was kind, generous, gentle, and always of good humor. She never had a bad day. If you were having a bad day and encountered Helen, your mood was instantly changed. Given the challenges in her life, it was shameful to be around her and be in a bad mood.

I think most of us did things for her. Open doors, carry books and lunch trays. I know I did. I would often walk with her to class, just to be sure she got there safely with few challenges.

On graduation day we held our breath as she climbed to the top of the rickety platform stairs with her diploma a short trek away. As she started to walk, all the graduates got to their feet and clapped, whistled, shouted and cheered. We were so happy for her. We all loved her. She was the most deserving of us all.

The Sign

As we were driving to the Graduation Ceremony, the maintenance team was just finishing the UMBC sign at the corner of Wilkens Avenue and Hilltop Road. I couldn't resist. I jumped out of the car, ran to the sign and jumped on top for a picture. Another car going to graduation almost crashed watching what I was doing.

After UMBC:

- Taught high school English
- Graduated from first class of the Baltimore International Culinary Arts Institute
- Work history of accounting, office manager, cooking in restaurants, sales in wine, hotel rooms and catering
- 1994 met Don (Donald) Hekler while taking courses at Landmark Education (formerly The Form and EST, which along with reading The Teachings of Abraham by Esther Hicks, altered my life.) and moved to Annapolis; married in 2004; no children
- Enjoys hobbies of wine tasting, cooking (founding member of La Confrerie de la Chaine des Rotisseurs, Baltimore Chapter, the oldest international food society), boating, and car enthusiast, especially F1 (Formula One) racing
- Attended the Monaco Grand Prix

A Sign of Graduation

This Belongs to Donna Helm '70, French

French Friends for Life

On the first day of school, 1966, it had been raining. I drove onto the parking lot and sat looking at the campus that I hoped would be my home for the next 4 years. I use the word campus loosely because all I could see was a sea of mud crisscrossed with plywood sidewalks. There was no landscaping, just 3 buildings in the distance. I got out of the car, wondering if this was someone's idea of a joke. I suddenly heard someone call my name. I turned and was surprised to recognize a classmate from junior high school, Midge Rohde. We were both glad to see a familiar face as we picked our way carefully across the slippery boards. As we walked towards the buildings I asked Midge if she had an idea of a major. She said she was undecided. I mentioned that I wanted to study French. At that she told me I needed to meet the friend who had driven with her who was also interested in French.

By now we had reached the first of the buildings. It housed the cafeteria on the ground floor and the gym above. The cafeteria would become the social gathering place in the absence of a student lounge. In the years to come many friendships would be forged there over the endless games of Hearts and Pitch. Across from this building was the theatre/lecture hall and ahead of us was Academic Building #1 which housed not only classrooms but faculty offices, a temporary library and the bookstore. Neither Midge nor I could have imagined in that moment the adventures that awaited us.

Over the next day or two I did meet Midge's friend, Louise Goodrich (Izat.) We spent the next 4 years studying French together, graduating together in June of 1970 and becoming best friends along the way. That friendship begun so long ago continues today and led us, in 2020 to endow a scholarship in memory of our beloved French Professor, Dr. May Roswell. I am grateful to UMBC not only for a wonderful education but for a lifelong friendship as well.

Team Spirit

Cheerleaders in 1967 looked very different than they do today. It was primarily a women's sport with few men to help with human pyramids and complex tumbling routines worthy of Olympic athletes. Our first squad was made up of 12 young women, some of whom had been high school cheerleaders and others who had not. We came together as a team to build spirit and a team following for our fledgling University. Not an easy task in an all-commuter school.

Our first uniforms were red and white, instead of the black and gold of today. We were trying to establish our individuality and distance ourselves from College Park. The uniforms were designed for us individually and made by a seamstress suggested by a squad member. They were lightweight wool and had to be dry cleaned. (What were we thinking?) Our routines were not the highly choreographed ones you see today. Rather most were adapted from routines from our various high schools. They involved lots of cartwheels and splits but few, if any, serious gymnastic moves. Our cheers were similarly adapted although eventually cheers were written specifically for UMBC.

Our first mascot was Sam, a live Chesapeake Bay Retriever. At one of our first soccer games I found myself picking Sam up to bring him to the game. Sam was a young, energetic and strong dog. I remember spending most of the game taking turns with other squad members running him up and down the sidelines to burn off some energy and tire him out. I don't know who was more tired at the end, the squad or Sam. I don't remember that he attended many games after that first one.

As a new school, our earliest win/loss records were not stellar but that certainly changed over the years. Today when I sit in our magnificent new arena and watch our mascot, cheer and dance squads at basketball games, it makes me smile to remember our earlier efforts at fostering team spirit.

After UMBC:

- Received Master's degree from Ohio State 1972
- Lived in Melbourne, Australia 1981-1985
- Career spent at John's Hopkins Bloomberg School of Public Health, Retired as Associate Dean 2006
- Married John Nolan 1978
- Served as first President Arbutus Senior Center 2010-2014
- UMBC Alumni Board 2016-2019
- Currently resides 6 months in Catonsville and 6 months in Portland, Maine

Go UMBC!

This Belongs to Marsha Herman '72, Psychology

Remembrance of my Time at UMBC

My time at UMBC coincided with an exciting time in women's rights, education, and life in general. We were eager for change and things were changing. What did it mean to be a woman in college, what could we look forward to in the future, what was happening in terms of equality? I looked around and saw we still lived in a patriarchal world, that options were limited, that gender bias was everywhere. But at UMBC, within those stark new brick buildings, I had the opportunity to work with some spectacular women, both educators and students.

Professor Nancy Henley was breaking the rules. Her views on grading and feminism were pulling us into a new future. When she explained that men touched women more often than women touched men, that the taboos about touch differed with gender, it rang true with us. It was something that we all lived but never had words for. In the hallway outside the psychology department office, she reached up, gently slapped the older male chair of the department on the back, curved her arm up and rested her hand on his shoulder. It was startling, a violation of the norms deeply inculcated in our gender and professional roles. I swear I can still hear the audible gasp of the students, teachers, and staff around her when she bravely reached out, and I can see the discomfort and confusion on the chair's face.

But this was important, a visual and tactile demonstration of how we were bound by the strictures and standards which delimited our freedoms. It was the beginning of awareness and change. Her views on grades, eliminating them in some classes, teaching us how to work for knowledge and not grades, impacted us by helping us develop reasons for learning other than attaining a good grade. I still remember one teaching strategy, using current events to explain psychological theories—I still remember the stories, all relevant to our understanding of the world. Most significantly, as her student, and as a woman, I was empowered by the way she led the way into a more gender fair world, and guided us to question the status quo.

Another excellent female professor of mine, Dr. Joan Rabin, had a different but equally pronounced impact on our views of ourselves as women. She was gentle in her approach, and approached learning with analytic and scientific precision. She showed her dedication to hearing what her female students said, encouraging us to use our brains, to offer our opinions, to read things in a different way, and not to be afraid of what it meant to be female, what it meant to be a bright woman, how to speak up without shouting but still be heard above the crowd. She brought her background in bio-psychology to bear on the emerging roles of women in society, and, like Dr. Henley, was on the vanguard of the nascent Women's Movement.

It was a privilege to be taught by these two stellar professors who helped encourage a generation of young women develop a strong sense of self, of personal strength, and direction during a time of great cultural turmoil. While my experience at UMBC was varied, and exciting, this factor, the way women taught us to embrace our power, is the most important thing I carry forward. Mentors seemed to be in short supply in many women's lives at that time, and I am grateful for having found two incredible mentors in my life, when I needed them. Their lifelong impact on me has been profound.

After UMBC:

- Earned doctorate in psychology
- Ready to retire from a career as a clinical psychologist in private practice
- Recently widowed, finding joy from memoir writing, and spending time with my two daughters, two granddaughters and friends
- Presently living in a Southern California beach town
- "I love taking long walks on the beach and taking photos, especially when extreme low tides coincide with sunset."

Dr. Janice Goldberg, Psychology

This Belongs to David R. Herron '71, Political Science

Photo Finish

When I was in high school, my only interests were photography, music, and girls (and not necessarily in that order). The result was that I had a D+ grade point average which was not good enough for a college prep diploma. I knew that I was not ready for college and decided to join the Navy either as a photographer or as a musician (I played string bass at that time and was pretty good, if I do say so myself!). I could not make up my mind between photography and music. So, I flipped a coin, and it came up photography. When one of my teachers found out what I had decided to do, he changed one of the grades he had given me so that I actually had a C- grade point average, which qualified me for a College Prep diploma.

So, on July 28, 1963, I found myself with a bunch of other boys on a train, heading from Detroit (my high school was in one of the suburbs, Royal Oak) to the Great Lakes Training Center just north of Chicago. Now in Navy boot camp a bunch of aptitude tests were thrown at me, to which I did not pay a great deal of attention.

When I sat down in front of the enlisted person who had the job and authority to decide what I would be doing for the next 3 years, he suggested that I might be better off becoming an aviation warfare technician, which surprised the hell out of me because it would require a lot of mathematics at which I had failed miserably in high school. So I told him that I wanted to become a photographer and if I could not get into that school, to send me to the fleet without any advanced training.

I found myself heading to Pensacola, Florida for the Navy's Photography school. When I arrived, I was called in by the Division officer who told me: "Herron, you're smart and if you don't get the highest grade in your class, it's because you are goofing off and you will be going to remedial classes in the evening." As it turns out, my roommate had already spent 6 years in the Navy and had re-enlisted for another 6 years on the condition that he could try the photography school. So, on the first exam, I scored 78% and my roommate scored 35%. We found ourselves in the evening remedial class together and ended up studying together as well. When my roommate scored high enough, I found myself scoring at least 90%! To celebrate, he would buy a couple of six packs of beer which we would drink out behind the barracks and get drunk!

I had never realized that I was smart until then. After that, the photography school was a breeze, and it was only a matter of time that I would decide to get out of the Navy and go to college.

By then, my parents had moved to Maryland where my father ended up working for Westinghouse near BWI. My oldest brother (who I knew was much smarter than me) had just graduated from College Park with a degree in Mathematics and had been an adjunct professor at UMBC the first year it opened, teaching mathematics. I had planned on going to College Park, but he convinced me that I would be much better off going to UMBC. So, I followed his advice and enrolled in the very first summer session in 1967.

I had decided to try to get two of the courses that I thought I would have the most difficulty with out of the way, Mathematics and Political Science. I do not remember who taught the Mathematics course, but the instructor for Political Science was Frank Burd, who had been an officer in the Air Force, and who had studied at the University of Chicago and was still writing his dissertation on Robert Taft. We spent practically the whole summer reading Aristotle's Politics. I will admit that I really did not understand much of what I read, but I was extremely flattered that Mr. Burd was challenging me. At the end of the summer session, there was only one exam, a final exam. When he handed the exam back to me, I could see that he had originally given me an A- but had crossed it out, replacing it with a B+. I confronted Mr. Burd about the grade change, asking him why he had changed the grade from an A- to a B+. His response was, "Mr. Herron, I think you are capable of doing much better and this is my way of encouraging you." And because of that, I became a Political Science major and eventually received a Ph.D. in that field.

After UMBC:

- Studied in France on and off from 1971 - 1975
- Earned PhD in Political Science 1987, Northern Illinois University
- Taught and did research for my dissertation on the Idea of Federalism in Western Europe
- Opposition Research for George Herbert Walker Bush for President campaign 1988-1989
- Political Appointee and Speechwriter to the Secretary of the Navy 1989 – 1991
- Maryland State Archives, Assistant Editor, Maryland Manual On-Line 1999-2015
- Berry Aneurysm Rupture, 1991
- Married Susan M. MacDonald, M.D. 1999 (Deceased 2020)
- Retired since 2015 and revived my interests in photography

This Belongs to Jim Hong '73, Biological Sciences

College Friends

The greatest memory is of the two close friends I made my sophomore year while taking science courses. Salvatore B. and Deena G. became close friends. We all commuted to school and had the same classes every morning. Most science majors had their afternoons occupied by the labs that went with the science courses. Almost every day we would meet for lunch in the cafeteria under the old Multi-Purpose building. We would discuss the classes and what one did not understand, the other two of us would attempt to explain in detail. This informal study group was great as we hardly ever had to study for exams and finals. Salvatore went on to work with the Maryland State Police in the Forensics Lab. Deena moved to Texas with her husband and I lost track of her.

Another memory happened one summer when I was working for one of the professors at school. I remember trying to get to campus for work, but it was right after Hurricane Agnes. On June 23, 1972 the hurricane had dropped so much rain the flooding was devastating. Since I lived in Glen Burnie at the time, I was going north on the west side of the Baltimore beltway (I695) to get to campus to go to work. I was stopped at the Patapsco River bridge, which had water running over it! Police directed me to turn around and go the wrong way down an entrance ramp to get back on the beltway to go back home.

There was a lot of unrest on campus in the early years. The Vietnam War was in full swing and the draft was in force. I do remember the Red Bricks underground campus paper and the occupation of the Administration Building (then Hillcrest House which has since been torn down) by groups of protesting students (me one of them). And ultimately the ordering of the National Guard onto campus to keep the peace and safety of the students. Seeing armed soldiers at the entrances to every building was a bit unnerving.

My last memory is of a close friend, John W. Even though he was an economics major we often would meet to chat, get a snack or walk between buildings. All I remember is him constantly complaining about hating economics! It finally got to be too much and I told him if he was that unhappy he should change majors. Well he finally did – to Chemistry! He went on to get a graduate degree and eventually worked for the Environmental Protection Agency.

Eventually my career led to working in Clinical Microbiology and Laboratory Management.

After UMBC:

- Completed internship in Medical Technology at The Medical Center at Princeton 1974
- Worked as a Bench Technologist for Anne Arundel Medical Center, and later the Pharmacokinetics Laboratory, University of Maryland School of Pharmacy.
- Supervisor of Clinical Microbiology and immunology, Memorial Hospital, York, PA.
- Supervisor and later Manager of the Clinical Microbiology and Infectious Diseases Laboratories of the University of Maryland Cancer Center.
- Senior Scientist and Database Administrator for the Phoenix Project Development Team at Becton Dickinson.
- Manager of Clinical Microbiology, Molecular Biology and Clinical Research at Quest Diagnostics Baltimore Business unit in Catonsville, MD.
- Technical Specialist, Clinical Microbiology and Infectious Diseases, Carolinas Medical System (now Atrium Health) based in Charlotte, NC.
- Retired 2017. Married 1975. Three children Jeremiah, Nathaniel and Alicia
- Enjoy biking the Greenways nearby on my road bike, and traveling to visit family
- "My education at UMBC exceptionally prepared me for graduate school as well as many career opportunities and advancements."
- Certified Specialist Clinical Microbiology 1991
- Graduate Degree in Clinical Microbiology, UMAB 1983

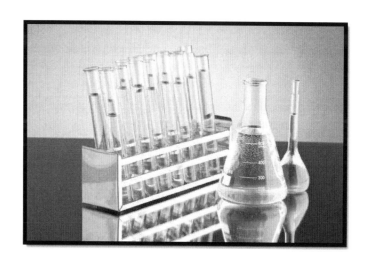

This Belongs to Mary Ogle Huebner '73, American Studies

Early Days at the UMBC Library

Everybody that went to UMBC in 1966 remembers the plywood 'sidewalks' and the mud. We were a brand new school with three buildings.

I checked with Simmona Simmons about the very early days of the UMBC library. She reminded me that the library started in Hillcrest in the summer of 1966, and moved to the Biology Building (or Academic One), when school started. The library was on the 3rd floor. The Director was John Haskell (the first full-time employee hired by Dr. Kuhn). From an article in the library's Special Collections room it stated that 'He spent many of the early months leading up to UMBC's opening ordering books, hiring new employees, and creating a catalog ordering system. Chancellor Kuhn's house served as the catalog center for the library's 20,000 volume collection...' The Assistant Director was Tony Raimo. John Haskell was a rather quiet Director, and Tony Raimo was quite the opposite. Other staff members were Sue Kemp (a librarian), and Simmona Simmons, Moses Wilson, and Kenneth Dean (non-professional staff). I worked there as a student assistant. Simmona was my boss. I cannot remember any other students who worked in the first library. I probably shelved a lot of books!!

The library stayed in the Biology building for about one year. Then it was moved into the 'new library' building (referred to as 'Phase One'). We used book trucks to move the books down the sidewalk by the pond.

I worked in the library as a student, but also became full time staff (not a librarian) somewhere around 1969. I worked in the Acquisitions Department. I believe Mr. Haskell left around the time we moved into the new library, and Tony Raimo became the Director. I definitely remember Mr. Raimo smoking cigars in the library (maybe not early on, but definitely in the 'new' library). Members of the professional librarian staff early on were Mary Louise Zeidel (Reference), Sue Kemp (Administration?), and Jim Reuter (Acquisitions?).

The student female staff were very close. We got together outside of the library for things like 'knitting bees,' movies, and other activities, and we all agreed that working in the library was our best job ever. Some of my student co-workers were Debbie Tinsley, Helen Riddle, Linda Weekly, Aldona Drazdys, Derryl Johnson and John Federline. Betty O'Neill, Blanche Staubs, and Mrs. Friedrich were full-time staff in processing and acquisitions.

I worked a lot with Gail Buffington in the Business Office, and her boss, Joan Pardoe. We had a great working relationship. Gail would send me notes with 'smiley faces' and funny notes, and I kept those notes for a very a long time.

I was raised a Catholic, and went to 12 years of Catholic school. The first 8 years were at St. Mark's, and the next 4 years were at Mt. de Sales (an all-girl school). Both schools were in the Catonsville area. I was in the last all-white class in both schools. So, when I got to UMBC, I was thrown into a whole new world, with African-Americans, Jewish people and...guys!!! And, of course, there were men teachers as well.

Most of my female classmates and I fell in love with Dr. Joel Jones, who taught English and American Studies. We were a tight knit group, and we had a baby shower for Dr. Jones and his wife, and I believe we also attended at least one party in their home. I'm sure it was because we were such a small campus and very close.

It was a special time, and I felt so lucky to be at UMBC. And having a job there, made it a really special experience.

And....it was the 60s! What a time....folk music (Hootenannies), the Viet Nam War and protests, Otis Redding actually performing at UMBC, just a wonderful time to be in college, and experience so many new things.

After UMBC:

- Received MLS (Master in Library Science) from UM School of Library Science
- First professional job as a Medical librarian at Peninsula General Hospital, in Salisbury, MD.
- Worked in a variety of libraries, including Public, (where I drove the Bookmobile); Director of Laurel Public Library, in Laurel, DE; Academic (Allegany Community College), and Prison (a maximum security prison in Cumberland, MD)
- Built and ran a B&B in Little Orleans, MD (near the C&O Canal). Catered to bicyclists riding the Canal from Cumberland to Washington, DC).
- Started (with the help of a retired history professor from Frostburg State University) a Lifelong Learning program for senior citizens, which is still going strong today!
- On the Board of two lifelong learning programs on the Eastern Shore, the local chapter of the State Bird Club, and the HOA where I now live.
- Moved to Salisbury in 1984, joined the Bird Club, and have been birding ever since. A reader, and volunteer at the local library and am in a book club in Laurel, DE.
- "I also love to drive to Assateague and walk the beach before the visitors get there!!"

This Belongs to Betty Huesman '70, American Studies

We Did It All

One of my favorite memories at UMBC is the inauguration of the women's sports program. Under the initiative and leadership of Linda (Lyall) Sowers a group of interested students launched three women's sports teams: basketball, volleyball and field hockey. Although many of us were not varsity-level high school athletes, what we may have lacked in exceptional talent we surpassed with enthusiasm, hard work and dedication. Due to the limited number of athletes in the early years, many of us played all three sports which led to a unique camaraderie. It was very gratifying to watch the competitive quality of the teams increase as the student population grew and the pool of experienced and talented athletes expanded.

After UMBC:

- Taught secondary-level English and Journalism in Baltimore County Public Schools 1970-1981
- Received Master of Liberal Arts, Johns Hopkins University 1973
- Studied computer programming at Catonsville Community College 1979-1981
- Information Technology Systems Developer and Technical Trainer 1981-2016
- Mother and grandmother: one daughter and a grandson

UMBC Field Hockey

This Belongs to David Insley '72, Interdisciplinary Studies

"Option 2" Degree

I entered UMBC with 15 transferable credits from Catonsville Community College in Fall of 1969. My main thought upon coming to UMBC was to go to this new school and get a liberal arts education, although at the time I had no real idea what my focus would be.

I lost my college enrollment status for the Selective Service and got drafted via the lottery that fall, but didn't pass the physical exam. Just that fast, my options for continuing at UMBC changed. There was no pressure to stay in school and get the "traditional" degree. Consequently, I ventured to try some something new in the spring. Enough of my brain cells were spent trying to conquer Calculus unsuccessfully.

Art classes won out. The Art Department faculty at the time, Leroy Morais and Pat Canavan, opened in me an awareness to another world. They took us to museums, showed us films and got us excited about things that I had only an inkling of previously. And to mix up the college experience more, anti-war protests escalated that spring 1970 and we were all cut loose from classes in April. Pass/ Fail became a grading option. UMBC seemed quite progressive.

Lee Morais gave filmmaking classes in fall 1970 and I was all in. This seemed like the career path I was looking for. At the time, there was no art or film degree offered at UMBC. I looked around at the few other colleges that offered film programs, but none were a feasible possibility for me. And anyway, I liked what was happening at UMBC. The variety of courses and events being offered was energizing.

I heard about the Option 2 program, now known as Interdisciplinary Studies, in which you could design and self–direct your own curriculum. This seemed perfect. A university being flexible with their curriculum was inspiring.

With Mr. Morais's help, I set to designing my Screen Arts Option 2 proposal. In addition to the filmmaking and film critique classes that were being offered at UMBC, we included courses in Theater, Music and aesthetics. We added Still Photography classes to be taken at Maryland Institute College of Art, since UMBC did not offer these at the time. There were also a number of Independent Project courses included one in which I would intern with working filmmakers and make my own films.

In Fall 1971, I presented my curriculum outline and objectives to a faculty panel. They had questions and suggestions, and after a week or two, they approved my Screen Arts Major. I believe I was one of the first Option 2 candidates. In summer 1972, I graduated with a BA in Screen Arts.

My time at UMBC was a great experience and a lot of fun. Previously unseen avenues of creative growth were everywhere. I've used this background for a successful 50 year career in the motion picture business as a cinematographer, and a fulfilling life so far.

So here's to UMBC - it's all your fault.
Thanks for being flexible.

After UMBC:

- Worked at UMBC Screen Arts Department Teaching Assistant '72- '75
- Itinerant Freelance Filmworker and Cinematographer 1972 -2017
- Director of Photography for 1000 TV Commercials.
- Feature films included John Waters' "Polyester", Hairspray", and "Crybaby".
- TV projects included "The Wire" from HBO, Blue Bloods (CBS) and "Person of Interest" (CBS).
- Married Joan DiSalvatore in 1971 (UMBC '74), Son Sam born 1980

Studio with Dr. Pat Canavan, Art

This Belongs to Louise Goodrich Izat '70, French

Increasing Vocabulary 101

I am part of an alumni committee where we reminisce a lot about our early days at UMBC. Many remember their first day, what they wore, and how their first classes went. Sadly, I seem not to remember very much from 50 years ago.

However, I do have one very vivid UMBC memory from an extraordinary day that feels like it was just yesterday. We held a protest on campus after the shooting at Kent State, and a large group of us marched afterward to the Catonsville Armory protesting the war in Vietnam. We all were chanting: "1,2,3,4, we don't want your f...king war; 5,6,7,8 remember Kent State". I remember being extremely uncomfortable saying that profanity out loud, but by the time we arrived at the armory, I was screaming the entire chant out loud just like everyone else.

What I remember most from that day was not that I increased my vocabulary of profanity, but feeling grown up and engaged, and a first-time feeling of being part of something bigger than we were; part of something we hoped might make a difference in the world. That day was an experience I will never forget and a feeling that still influences me today.

After UMBC:

- 25 year Human Resources career with Department of Defense Research and Development Center
- Married Paul Izat, 1985; both loving travel, took many trips vacationing abroad whenever possible
- Upon retiring, was blessed to babysit two young cousins and was caregiver to my mother for ten years
- Re-connected with fellow alumni in 2015; learned what wonderful things UMBC had to offer and discovered the fun of attending UMBC events such as concerts, Homecoming, fundraisers, etc.
- Lives in Glen Burnie and enjoys volunteering in church community outreach activities and programs

Anti-War Protest

This Belongs to Beverly Rankin James '70, Sociology

Fostering Lifelong Friends

What can be said about my experience as a student at the University of Maryland Baltimore County (UMBC) for four years from 1966 to 1970/1971?

I have always been proud to be a UMBC graduate and will not hesitate to say I am an alumna when the conversation comes up. As a graduate in the 1970/71 classes with bachelor's degrees in Sociology and Social Work, let me start there to express my good fortune to have been a student at this university. The university was unique in that it offered a degree in social work which was my choice of major and unique because the specific courses to attain a social work degree were not offered by most other colleges or universities at that time. When I graduated in 1970 my degree was in Sociology only because a degree in Social Work was not offered at that time. However, it was offered in the succeeding year of my graduation, and I returned to complete 10 additional credits and receive a degree in social work. I believe this degree enhanced my ability to get my first post graduate job in my chosen field as a Social Worker since I was immediately offered a position at Baltimore City Hospitals (currently Johns Hopkins Hospital/Bayview) as a Social Worker. After two years of employment, I resigned to continue my education. I was offered a full scholarship to attend the University of Pennsylvania School of Social Policy and Practice (Formerly University of Pennsylvania School of Social Work). Again, a step I believe was actualized due to my history that included being a graduate of UMBC. The university continues to grow with excellent staffing, extensive facilities and trailblazing academia.

I enrolled at UMBC after the recommendation from my Western High School counselor in Baltimore MD. The tuition was affordable for an African American Baltimore City female resident whose goal was to continue her education by attending college. I was excited to attend UMBC because it was a new university as opposed to Morgan and Coppin which were the expected schools to attend. Also, the school was accessible meaning I could continue to live at home, I could travel there by using public transportation and I could afford the tuition on part-time employment.

This is where I will start to begin to share with you what my experience was like as an UMBC student. My classes started at 8am in the morning and I needed to use two buses or connecting buses to get to the campus. When I traveled as far as I could on the bus, I was still at least three blocks from the campus buildings where the classes were held. This three-block area was not a paved walkway but a grass field that was not shielded by buildings that would block the wind on those very cold early mornings as you tried to get to class on time. I valued being on time and was on time for my classes, but public transportation, cold winters and unpaved access made this venture a very tall order. Of course, how I came to campus was also how I left campus meaning the use of public transportation impacted how long in each day I would remain on campus.

I just used the word "campus" several times. The campus was three buildings: the Lecture Hall, Academic Building #1, and the Multipurpose Building which included a cafeteria. The limited number of facilities also impacted the amount of time I spent on campus. When I was on campus but did not have a class or I was between classes I spent a good amount of time playing cards and engaging with other students in that first year of college life. The time in the Student Union changed after the first year and the receipt of my grade point average. My grades were lower than I expected. After that I spent much less time in the Student Union and more time in the Multipurpose Building where I used the time to study. I felt the professors were very dedicated and well versed in their field. I felt they wanted the students to do well but it was fully the student's responsibility to make that happen. My least accomplished class was music, strange but true.

When I arrived on campus, I did not know anyone else. I was looking forward to the opportunity to get to meet new people especially African American people. I learned that there were seven hundred and fifty students enrolled. Of these students, nineteen were African American and eleven were female. These numbers were of course far fewer than I had anticipated but I was able to foster lifelong friends with three other African American students that became family friends where we raised our children together and/or shared our lives until today. Also, I bonded with many of the African American students in the efforts to increase the numbers of African American students enrolled at UMBC by participating in the development and implementation of the Black Student Union.

One of the highlighted experiences in being a student at UMBC was enrolling in a class during what was call the "MiniMester". The MiniMester was a six-week period between the end of the fall semester and the beginning of the spring semester. During this period in January 1969 a class in ancient history was offered and I enrolled. This was a three-week student paid class to travel to England, France and Italy for the visual effects of ancient history. This class through UMBC exposed me to experiences and situations that I had not had before. I had never been away from home independently; I had not previously flown on a plane, and I had not seen the coliseum in Rome and the many other visits made on this trip.

The campus continued to grow and expand while I was there with additional buildings and students. By then I was more focused and definitive in the use of my time. Although I never felt I would not graduate I always worked to make sure I did.

After UMBC:

- Received Masters in Social Work at the University of Pennsylvania School of Social Policy and Practice in 1975
- Worked as a Medical Social Worker at BayView Hospital (formerly Baltimore City Hospital) for two years
- Worked at the Baltimore City Head Start administrative office as the Parent Involvement/Social Work Specialist for eighteen years
- In 1993, worked for Catholic Charities as the Director of the Herring Run Head Start Program which served 102 children and their families
- In 2000, began work for the Annie E Casey Foundation/Casey Family Services for ten years as a Program Team Leader
- Married in 1976 and celebrated 46 years this March 6th. We have one son and one granddaughter
- Retired, traveled extensively for pleasure, and remain an active tennis player to this day

Bon Voyage, January 1969

This Belongs to Gale Ortgies Johnk '71, English

Close Faculty Friends

I had had a year at College Park, where as another alumnus mentioned, there were classes on television and in lecture halls that held up to 500 students. I recall some of the courses I took, including my first German class, but I remember nothing about the professors, and there was no relationship with any of them.

At UMBC, the relationship between students and professors is something that really stands out. I went to parties at the homes of Jim Arnquist and Tom Benson. A lot of the professors joined us in the moratorium that took place as a protest against the war. I was close enough to some of the instructors, that three of them were invited to our wedding. That close contact made for excellent class discussions, which often spilled over into the faculty offices. The ancient history teacher was very interesting, and interested me in a subject that I had not previously enjoyed. I still recall the roll out of his Battle of Thermopylae presentation. Mary Kleinhans was one of my favorite English teachers, and she was one of the people at our wedding. Janet Carsetti also came; Tom Powers was invited but couldn't come. Anyway, it suffices to say that the quality of education was really top notch in my view, and the relationship with teachers was nurturing and inspiring. I also remember the rumor that it was being prepped as a grad school for U of Md., but never knew whether or not that was substantiated by fact.

Sue Frankford was my closest friend after Jimmy. She took 18 credits every semester, and finished her credits in December of 1970, a full semester ahead. Of course, she was also younger than the rest of us. She took 18 more credits "for fun" and studied everything, including Latin and Greek. She took the class trips to Rome and Athens as part of those courses. She was the most forward thinking person I think I ever met and was way ahead of her time. She was the editor for the 1971 yearbook, and I do have that yearbook. When she died, she was on her way to Boston to become the assistant to Nancy Henley, a sociology teacher from UMBC; at that point, Sue wasn't even 21.

This Belongs to Art Kahn '70, Psychology

Reflecting Back, Looking Forward

Our 50th Reunion being abruptly snatched from our calendars due to a global pandemic was a huge disappointment. Sharing memories and life events in person would have been rewarding. So here I am, remembering those inaugural campus years with fondness, realizing they hopefully set a direction for each of us to pursue personally going forward. But I also recognize that we, as the 'pioneering' class, played an integral part in shaping UMBC's first baby steps toward the world class university it is today.

Coming from all-male Baltimore City College HS, I chose UMBC to provide a real-world academic experience, but in a campus setting uniquely small by college standards, avoiding being just another number at a large college. That we comprised the first student body was a rare and unique opportunity. Ironically, I noted that a significant number of fellow freshmen in 1966 had also come from local all-girl or all-boy schools, in many ways, putting us in the 'same boat'. Over those next four years, many of us nurtured friendships, growing both from our similarities and differences. It was a special time. It was a trying time. It was The Sixties. Our years at UMBC were marked by world events which, in many ways, influenced our lives going forward. Bobby Kennedy, Martin Luther King, Kent State, Vietnam, Chicago Seven, Military Draft, Woodstock, Moon Landing. On a lighter note locally, there were the indignities of the Lost 1969 Championships – Mets over the Orioles in the World Series, Jets over the Colts in the Super Bowl.

Yet, back on campus, memories were plentiful. Registration at Hillcrest using IBM punch cards, working in the UMBC Library on the 3rd Floor of the Academic Building, hanging out at The Switchboard and the Bookstore. Reading 'The Retriever'. Psychology classes with Janis Goldberg and Lowell Groninger, Sociology with Bill Rothstein. Bantering with Campus Officer McCubbin. Watching Bill Morgenstern photographically capture seemingly every moment and event of UMBC's first years, Christmas caroling at Maiden Choice Shopping Center, co-planning UMBC's First Graduation.

All-in-all, the pioneering aspect of our inaugural four years at UMBC, both 'growing' the campus, and 'growing' ourselves was a special, and somewhat challenging time. Looking back, it was a unique opportunity, priceless in its accumulation of moments, memories and friendships that we shared, and hopefully are still able to cherish a half-century later and beyond.

After UMBC:

- Worked for Social Security Administration 1972 to 2013
- In my free time pursued life-long interest in photography
- During 1970's and 80's, explored Chesapeake Bay region, capturing vanishing Maryland scenes and images
- Photos included in exhibit sponsored by Chesapeake Bay Maritime Museum
- Participated in Sunny Sundays program at the then 'new' Inner Harbor, as well as in numerous regional arts and ethnic festivals
- Married in 1977, daughter born in 1985, and awaiting birth of a grandchild
- Still living in Baltimore area

Campus Construction During Classes, 1966

This Belongs to Louis Klein '70, Biological Sciences

For the Love of the Game

My purpose in choosing UMBC was twofold. Firstly, it was a vast savings over a multitude of university choices. Secondly, there was a possibility of continuing my football career.

I went to Baltimore City College High School. It was the alma mater for my father and my pediatrician who took care of me up until I was 21. I was excited thinking I was going to the school my father attended, and I was going to play football. On my very first day, I was walking up the long, long path from 33rd Street to the huge portal, and there in front of me was the BCC BAND! I was scared to death seeing what I was seeing. The huge number of band members all older than me! The sound! The band frightened me and then I became too scared to try out for football. So I sat out my freshman year due to fear. If the band was that big, can you imagine the size of the players? I didn't stand a chance.

In 1963, I attended the annual City-Poly football game and watched my team get beat. I sat in the stands at Memorial Stadium and lowered my head. I swore at that moment I was going to play for BCC. Fear had no place in my thinking while seated at that game. I was determined to make a change. So long story short, I played for 2 years on the Varsity Team and was going both ways, offense and defense. The final game was the payoff. It was Thanksgiving Day 1965. We defeated Poly for second year in a row at Memorial Stadium for the Maryland Scholastic Associations "A" Conference Championship. It was a Cinderella story of sorts. I was picked by the Associated Press for the All-Maryland Scholastic Associations' Football Team.

I never had real notoriety until that game. Better late than never, I guess. From that performance I was offered a letter of intent by Western Maryland College to play football. But, the caveat was that I had to study what they wanted me to study. I wanted Medicine and that was out of the question. So I chose UMBC. Pre-Med here I come.

I loved Medicine. Maybe, I could also have football success at UMBC. Rumor had it when I arrived that they were having a meeting to organize a football team. Wow. What an opportunity. Pre-med and Football. Who knew? So I showed up!

I was determined to be the first student to walk through the door of the first football meeting at Hillcrest. I was that first student. I remember it clearly. A conference room with a large table. When I sat down and other students wandered in gradually, I was informed by Del Langdon, the coach, that it was a meeting for the First Lacrosse Team, not football. So I figured, it looks like I am going to play Lacrosse. How am I going to do that?

The rest is history. I played four years of Varsity Lacrosse in the starting defense. It was a fabulous journey. I remember everything to this day and will never forget. Although I didn't play in a stadium with 26,000 football fans, I played with a group of student athletes whom I respected for their skill and friendship. I learned the game from them. I learned the game from my coaches. I played. I played "For the Love of the Game."

After UMBC:

- For 20 years, served as a combat medic/ medical corpsman and Physical Therapist in the US Army National Guard and US Army Reserve. Retired as Major.
- Developed with my wife the first Private Physical and Occupational Therapy Practice specializing in rehabilitation of the Hand and Upper Extremity in the San Francisco Bay Area (1977 to 2003). I continue to work as a Doctor of Physical Therapy and Rehabilitation.
- Continued my Sports Medicine interests by serving as consultant and trainer to my children's sports teams over the years and various high schools in the Bay Area and San Francisco State University.
- Consulted to the Oakland As, Golden State Warriors, and San Francisco 49ers, and the producers of Angels in the Outfield.
- My plan is to continue my work and move on to Doctors Without Borders
- Married Elizabeth Cauldwell. We lost Beth to cancer in 2005, but she lives on with her legacy, three wonderful children and three grandchildren.
- To quote Rudy from the movie, "Chase that stupid dream.... it can be done!"

UMBC Lacrosse, 1969

This Belongs to Fran (Frances) Douthirt Kormann '70, Psychology

Making it Happen

In 1965, my senior year of High School, I was excited to hear that University of Maryland would open a campus near my Halethorpe home, making it possible for me to afford college because…. I could live at home. I was one of six kids, so receiving financial aid was critical for me to attend college. When accepted at UMBC I was offered work on campus as a secretary assisting Sharon Sekulich through the Work/Study Program. Sharon was the department secretary for all the Biology and Chemistry professors. Dr. Konetzka, Chairman of the Biology Department and Sharon Sekulich were so supportive and provided me with flexible work hours to help pay my tuition. Our office was on the second floor of the Academic Building which was the only constructed office/classroom building on campus when the school opened in September 1966. So, anything and everything that was happening took place in the Academic Building – with a carefully balanced walk on a wood plank walkway to the gym and cafeteria. Everything a student needed.

Ceil – the campus switchboard operator – was on the fourth floor of the Academic Building. Ceil had an open-door policy, and a large green couch where all the working students would gather throughout the day to get her friendly advice about life. Ceil multitasked as a talented telephone switch board operator and college shrink for overwhelmed students. I met my lifelong friend Mimi Dietrich on Ceil's green couch. Mimi was also a working student who worked with Ceil as a telephone switchboard operator. Many of us worker bees gathered around Ceil to relax and socialize. Her nurturing spirit and sense of humor was refreshing and memorable.

My high school did not have any athletic programs and I was anxious to try college sports. Being in a new University with only a couple hundred first year students, there were many opportunities to play sports. I played field hockey and basketball. Of course, I did not know any of the rules, but the coaches and spectators were incredibly supportive. I was "recruited" for Basketball by Louie (Linda Lyall), a talented basketball player, who was adamant about starting a women's basketball team. I met her near the gym, and she asked me if I wanted to play basketball. I explained that I did not know anything about the sport, and she said, "all I need is someone to fill a shirt." So, I was now a basketball player! Being a newbie to the sport I did not get much of a chance to play. Until…. One night the crowd (prompted by friends) started chanting "we want Fran." The coach obliged and let me play and much to the crowd's pleasure, I scored a basket. Thus, my college athletic career is a great memory for many.

I was a Psychology major and so was Frank Kormann. Frank and I met in our Junior Year in the back row of our Abnormal Psychology class. Dr. Goldberg frequently asked us if we were there to hear her lecture or had other motivations. In our Senior Year, the draft lottery launched for the Vietnam war. We spent months discussing what to do if Frank's "number" (his birthdate) was drawn. Studying was on the back burner as we waited for the day of the drawing. It was a numbing feeling when Frank's number was drawn. Rather than be drafted with no choices, he chose to enlist right after graduation. Because of the Vietnam War and the draft lottery, our Senior Year was a sad and scary time as we prepared for a lot of unknowns.

Frank and I married two months after graduation in August 1970 between his completion of boot camp and his deployment to Korea (not Vietnam) 51 years ago. We are married alums who have a wonderful family, had successful careers and are now enjoying an active retirement life. We are extremely grateful for all the comradery and support we received from professors, university staff, friends, and those who supported our Work/Study program which made our education happen. We are proud alums of the first graduating class of UMBC.

After UMBC:

- Realtor in Rochester New York and Northern Virginia for 40 years. Retired.
- Loudoun County Community Ambassador Volunteer Since 2018
- 2019 Loudoun County Senior Volunteer of the Year
- Married 1970 to Frank Kormann class of UMBC 1970
- 2 Children, 5 Grandchildren.
- Lives in Leesburg VA

UMBC Women's Basketball Goes for the Score

This Belongs to Frank Kormann '70, Psychology

Mascot Retriever Sam Attends his First Basketball Game

It all came back to me on March 16, 2018. On that day, the #16 seed Retrievers defeated the #1 seed Cavaliers in the first round of the NCAA Men's Basketball Tournament. Everyone was shocked, surprised, and proud of our Retrievers. My mind drifted back to another exciting men's basketball game about 50 years earlier in 1968 in the original gym…

I was a full-time student working part-time for Dean of Faculty Homer W. Schamp and Secretary Mary Jane Randolph in the Hillcrest Building. At that time Hillcrest housed all the campus administration offices, including Director of Physical Plant Guy Chisolm. Everyone was excited when Guy Chisolm announced the first Chesapeake Bay Retriever puppy mascot - Sam - had arrived. Sam lived at the Chisolm family home on campus.

Before long, everyone wanted to see and play with Sam. Someone in the office suggested that Sam attend the next men's basketball game. I recall Mr. Chisolm was less than enthusiastic about the idea but asked for a volunteer. I jumped at the opportunity. I envisioned a fun 15-minute hike from the Chisolm home to the gym, where Sam would be introduced to the crowd at half-time and then a pleasant return. I was familiar with dogs—but not 'Chessies.'

Sam was a typical Chessie pup, with unbridled energy and a loud bark; incapable of staying still and convinced that everyone and everything was for his entertainment. As I approached the Chisolm backyard, I heard Sam barking and howling with anticipation. My first inkling of doubt came as I tried to attach the leash. Sam was excited! Leash on! Sam did not understand the purpose of a leash.

For the next 30 minutes I wrangled Sam across the field to the gym. I was relieved. Sam was excited! I did not envision what happened next. Picture a crowded home gym, students cheering, game in progress…and then someone walks in with an 'adorable' young pup on a leash. Students swarmed wanting to pet Sam. The 'adorable' pup began barking, jumping with excitement, spinning like a whirling dervish. I felt the eyes of the spectators shift from the game to the commotion at the gym entrance. Somehow Sam was drawing even more energy from the crowd.

In the office two days later, I recounted the events to Mr. Chisolm. He thanked me for getting Sam out of the gym before the officials could stop the game. Recalling that conversation, I am certain Mr. Chisolm was stifling a grin.

A Tell Tale Tour of Hillcrest

The early Skipjack yearbooks include photographs of the exterior of Hillcrest building, the administrative hub of our new university campus. Dean of Faculty and Vice Chancellor Homer W. Schamp was located on the second floor. I recall student and other administrative offices were on the first floor. And the basement level housed the Physical Plant Department, Engineering, Security, multilith printing machine, computer room…and OFF LIMITS--DO NOT ENTER the rear of the basement…

I operated the campus multilith printing machine for Dean Schamp and Secretary Mary Jane Randolph. Every day I was up and down--second floor to basement and back again—completing print jobs and maintaining that quirky machine. And every day I saw the OFF LIMITS—DO NOT ENTER sign posted at the rear of the basement! One might think such a commanding sign would be on a locked door. But I do not recall any locked door…just a doorway maybe…and the sign taunting me on every trip to the basement.

Growing up locally, I was aware of Spring Grove Hospital. I 'learned' the anecdotal 'history' of Hillcrest as part of Spring Grove and also noted it was a distance from the main hospital grounds. Rumors about Spring Grove were rampant in the community. And Hillcrest, formerly a Spring Grove facility, was now the administrative center of our new campus. What was in the rear of the basement? One day the sign was gone…or I didn't see it…or I didn't read it. Okay, I ignored it!

A large open room, pieces of old furniture, incredibly quiet…and multiple smaller rooms. Solid steel doors with small viewing windows, padded walls and floors, and silence. I was in a 'treatment' facility, a solitary confinement ward, completely empty, no sign of past use. Did I mention it was incredibly quiet? I imagined times past when it may not have been so quiet. In some small way, this experience sparked my curiosity. Psychology Professor Janice Goldberg became a favorite teacher. And I graduated with a degree in Psychology.

Working for Vice Chancellor and Dean of Faculty Homer W. Schamp

First day of college life. Exploring the campus did not take long: three buildings, piles of dirt and mud. Managed to find the cafeteria…tables, chairs, and vending machines…and a bulletin board advertising jobs on campus! I needed money for tuition! I filled out the form and posted it on the board. Next day my form was missing. I repeated the process. Within a day or two, Mary Jane Randolph requested I come to her office in Hillcrest for an interview.

Mrs. Randolph was secretary to Dean of Faculty and Vice Chancellor Homer W. Schamp. She had retrieved my "missing" form that first day. Over the next four years, I worked 20 hours a week for Dean Schamp and Secretary Randolph at

Hillcrest. Dean Schamp was responsible for recruiting all the initial faculty. I witnessed a man, free of ego, accept every challenge with a sense of humor and determination to succeed. He was soft-spoken and respected by every member of faculty and staff.

Mary Jane Randolph functioned like a Chief of Staff. To my knowledge, she never failed to meet a deadline even as she and Dean Schamp accepted more and more responsibility. In hindsight, my functional education began with that first interview, only a day or two after my academic education started.

The office work environment was very inclusive. Over the years Dean Schamp's office staff grew to include three student workers and the registration and counseling staff. We worked, we laughed, we problem-solved together. I recall working, running down the hill to class, and rushing back uphill to the aptly named Hillcrest for more work.

The student body was growing each year, and the campus administrative processes had to evolve as well. One year, we realized the class scheduling and student registration process was faltering. And in the Hillcrest basement sat a new, gleaming, recently installed Univac computer.

Our office was convinced that a computer could solve our scheduling and registration challenge. First, we had to convert all the forms to 'IBM cards'…but we did not have any keypunch machines. My father ran the data processing department at Baltimore Gas and Electric. BGE had progressed beyond manual keypunching and delivered a room full of surplus keypunch machines to UMBC. Our students worked for hours diligently keypunching all the data onto cards— only to discover our new computer was 'down.'

Judith Hirsch worked in our office as Counselor and Scheduling Officer. She cajoled an associate at the College Park campus to 'run' our program. College Park agreed, but only had a small time-window available. I borrowed Miss Hirsch's car and raced boxes of 'IBM cards' to College Park. The next day I returned to College Park and raced boxes of printouts back to Miss Hirsch at UMBC. I recall that somehow everything worked.

And I learned that even a part-time student worker could make a significant difference. My experience in that office environment had a positive impact on my life. My UMBC degree is valuable. My exposure to teamwork, problem-solving, mutual respect, professional pride, and personal accomplishment at UMBC is invaluable.

After UMBC:

- United States Army veteran
- MBA College of William and Mary
- United States Postal Inspector retired

- Realtor in Northern Virginia retired
- Married 1970 to Fran Douthirt, UMBC Class of 1970
- Enjoys family and grandchildren, biking, boating and traveling

Sam, UMBC's First Live Mascot

This Belongs to Nancy Krebs '72, Theater

The Curtain Goes Up!

I have so many stories, and fond memories of the young UMBC that had in my Freshman year only 3 buildings on the campus, connected by muddy planks that served as walkways. Other buildings were being constructed all around us, and it was a noisy, exciting time. In my Freshman year, I began to take classes in the Theatre Department under the leadership of Dr. Alice Robinson. At that time there was no 'theater' per se, just Lecture Hall 1 -which served a variety of purposes, not the least of which was as the venue for all the productions created by our fledgling department, which was initiated in 1966-1967, I think. I could be wrong....but in my first and second years, I performed in Stop the World, I Want to Get Off, Rumpelstiltskin, Spoon River Anthology and an original rock musical-- Keep the Peace, Baby, for which I wrote the musical score and lyrics. I was only 18 years old. Clyde Rader was the director for several of these, and I do believe that Dr. Robinson directed a production of Antigone - remember watching it in the lecture hall.

As the campus buildings grew in number--the Student Union with it's small theater housed our growing department, and Bill Brown joined the faculty as Technical Director and taught all the Stagecraft classes, Will Hicks was the Acting instructor, Dr. Robinson still taught Theatre History, Readers Theatre, Oral Interpretation among other courses. The faculty continued to grow throughout my four years there.

All in all, I performed or participated in over 14 productions while at UMBC, and my training there laid the foundation for my professional career in the Theatre and Performing Arts. I cherish my time spent there and the memories of those early years.

After UMBC:

- Attended the Dallas Theater Center for graduate studies in Acting
- Professional actor/singer/musician 1975-present. Owner/Operator of The Voiceworks 1994-present. Taught for 39 years at the Baltimore School for the Arts, Theatre Department
- Married Byron 'Pete' Baden in 1983, widowed in 2012
- Named a Lessac Master Teacher in 2002, teaching voice/body training globally
- Currently the Resident Voice/Dialect Coach for The Classic Theatre of Maryland and coaches various professional theatre companies in the region and acting professionally as well.
- Music Minister for various churches since 1994
- Currently living in the Severn area

This Belongs to Jeanette Lampron '70, History

Deciding to go to UMBC

When I was a senior in high school my father was typical of many who did not want to "waste" money on college for a daughter who was only going to get married. The only option, it seemed to me, was to enlist in the service in order to get my education. I went to the DC Air Force recruiting office and met a Sgt. Foster. After taking the test I was accepted into the nursing program at Walter Reed. Papers in hand I told my dad. He was furious. He refused to sign them. In those days a girl needed to be twenty one to make any decisions about her life. A boy only needed to be eighteen.

I said then that I wanted to go to college. No. So, I looked into UMCP and found out that it was $150 a semester plus books. I figured that I might be able to afford it on my dental assistant job at minimum wage that I'd had since I was fifteen.

A boyfriend said that he was going to a brand new school that was part of the University of Maryland and it was $25 a semester cheaper. Not only that, if you paid for the semester you could take as many classes as you could handle. You could also participate in a new January semester and pick up more credits. Year around school!

I went to my dad and told him about it.

He said that if I paid my own way, took care of my own personal and car expenses and paid $15 a week toward room and board, he'd allow me to do it until I was 21. Ok!

I went over to the old house and literally just walked into Dr. Kuhn's office. I introduced myself and he instantly became my mentor. The first semester was rough for me. After that, I took as many as 21 credits and graduated in three years without any debt and having paid my weekly room and board.

Two years later my dad gave all that money back to me to do what I wanted for a wedding or for getting started. He was really proud of me.

UMBC afforded me an opportunity for which I am grateful for to this day. Dr. Kuhn will always be in my heart too.

Classes

Growing up I went to parochial schools for all but one semester of eighth grade. When we moved to Maryland my parents could not convince the local Catholic school to take me for that short period of time, so I attended Anne Arundel Jr. High.

When I got to UMBC, the classroom building was smaller than that school by a huge margin of space!

If I remember correctly, the top floor was for faculty offices and most of the classrooms I frequented were on the first floor. At one end was an elevator that never seemed to run properly. It groaned. It stalled. It jerked to a stop. It reminded me of the elevator in a Mary Tyler Moore/Julie Andrews movie that I had just seen - Thoroughly Modern Millie. In the movie they would dance to get the elevator to move.

On the very first day at UMBC I had an 8am English 101 class. As the professor called roll I heard the name of a girl who I knew of but had never met for years. People kept saying that I must meet her! When I heard her name I turned around to see her waving at me.

After class we met and talked until everyone else had gone. We got on the elevator. It started its antics. At the very same time we both started to dance. Barbara Plowman, now Filar, was maid of honor at my wedding and best friend for life.

UMBC provided so many wonderful lifelong friends and memories. Even the memory of an improperly installed elevator brings a smile to my face.

Student Teaching

The fall of 1969 was preparation time for student teaching. I was one of four classmates who had chosen high school in Howard County. We were all assigned to go to the new school, Atholton.

The very fact that we had preparatory sessions was rather novel. The fact that we had to develop lessons and teach them in a video-taped session that included students who had to recruit for a "class", was revolutionary.

Watching my tape was incredibly instructive. My nervousness showed. I twisted the chord to the microphone over and over and made so many mistakes. Dr. Neville was so kind in helping me to interpret what I saw and was so encouraging.

That preparatory class and the support of my supervising professor, made it possible for me to get a job in the county and stay there until 2013.

Graduation

Graduation was incredibly complicated for me. Being on the graduation committee was to be in a difficult situation. It was important to me that everyone be listened to and respected. Because of the political situation, demonstrations and protests of various kinds were bound to occur. I fielded many calls from various protest groups at other campuses, including most Ivy League schools. How they got my home phone number I will never know. When we met with the class for an information session I tried to share that information. Whether I agreed or disagreed had no bearing to me. I felt required to share it. I was practically booed off of the stage but someone stepped in to hush the group, saying that I was just sharing information.

At the same time the weather was creating problems of its own for me and the committee. Storms were forecast for the day. Dr. Kuhn really wanted to have the ceremony moved inside. I and others begged to just have the option there in case it did start to rain before the ceremony.

He was wonderful, allowing us to make that plan with him. He didn't have to do that. As I walked across the stage and he congratulated me he leaned forward and smiled saying something to the effect that even the weather couldn't argue with me.

As it turned out the man I married was related to him by marriage and we lived nearby. What a gift.

After UMBC:

- Received M.A. from Castleton State College (VT) 1980
- Taught middle school for thirty years and mentored social studies teachers for eleven years
- Teacher Historian of the Year for Howard County - National Capitol Historic Society 1989
- Frequent curriculum writer and presenter at National Council for Social Studies
- Co-authored Out of Slavery, a curriculum guide, with Susan Denhart Apple, another UMBC graduate, for the Maryland Historical Society
- Currently a travel advisor
- Married Robert Botterill in 1972. Two children. Regina and Jason and their spouses and six grandchildren.

This Belongs to Lois Bleifus Vargas Blake Lee '73, Psychology

Making Life Changes

At age 26, I found myself interviewing for a secretarial position with the chairman of the UMBC education division. Little did I know this would turn a corner in my life's Journey. Working with that divisional faculty helped me develop confidence and learn to risk. I began taking classes in multiple departments ultimately graduating with an English major. My UMBC experience stimulated new ways of thinking through a different method of instruction-not just passively absorbing facts but instead learning to grasp what the student could do with this knowledge. I wasn't unique! If one follows the reports of years of alumni, evidence of this educational path set many on the road to ultimate success. Faculty, staff, students and even a janitor turned everyday life events into self-growth. Now, reviewing letters written decades ago, one can see how faculty exuded encouragement, challenging students to achieve their own individual destiny. Yes, I remember you and the spirits of those who have passed to another realm too.

Some of you may not know that part of the UMBC campus was previously a facility housing the chronically mentally ill. In fact, in the basement of the admin building on the hill, an old cell (complete with bars!) had been used to restrain out of control patients—clearly a symbol of inhumanity to those affected by this illness. Ironically, my professional life choices stemmed from that moment on—later opting to spend over thirty years as a mental health professional focusing on compassionate treatment for those so afflicted.

During these early years college campuses were afire with values-conflict. The Vietnam War erupted into demonstrations and heated discussions. Students morphed from recipients of academia into citizens of the world. From these early years, it became clear UMBC was destined to attract the gifted to become an honors university. Was this clear in the recruitment of its unique faculty?

My experience on the education student advisory council and editor of that newsletter may have influenced my future literary product forms. Indeed it seems that those professors who shared their humanness, goal-nurturing and intellectual acumen with their students have seeded countless growth to our society at large.

These past fifty-three years have found me professionally (and as an avocation) engaged in community service, authoring multiple newsletters, periodicals and books. Likewise, I have been involved in the musical, artistic, writing, teaching, and mental health growth of children and adults. It has been a great life and I hope it is not over yet. Thanks for offering us the opportunity to say hello to our pasts and hope for our futures. Thanks for being there for all of us!

After UMBC:

- Received MA in clinical psychology Towson State U. 1977
- Served 30 years as mental health professional/administrator in Pennsylvania, Alaska, and Washington state
- Wrote books about Native American culture in Washington, and co-authored book on funding for visual artists, published poetry
- International musical co-founder toured Japan, Quebec, Chile, Russia and US
- Active community service for decades: mental health statewide leader, historical society, community centers and social service group presidents
- Married three times, widowed twice. Adopted three children: Fiona, Stephanie and Joseph

Dr. Bettridge, English, Lectures about Beowulf

This Belongs to Bruce Lippmann '72, Social Work

Wrestling First

I graduated in the Class of 1972. Majored in Sociology and Social Work. I helped organized the first Chapter of the National Association of Student Social Workers at UMBC and was its first President.

But, in the Fall of 1971, UMBC began its first wrestling team. I wrestled in the 126 lb. weight class. We were in the Mason-Dixon Conference. My wrestling partner was Harley Feldberg, who wrestled at 118 lbs. That's a weight class that's no longer in existence in the NCAA's. For a first year team, we did ok. Both Harley and I were Co-Captains and we both placed 4th at the Mason-Dixon Wrestling Championships held at Western Maryland College in February 1972. Harley and I were Co-MVP's of this first team. Many fond memories of my two years at UMBC.

After UMBC:

- Started U of Md School of Social Work in Sept 1972 but ended up getting drafted into US Army. Served in US Army Oct 4, 1972 to Oct 5, 1975 as Behavioral Science Specialist. Discharged Honorable with Meritorious Service Award as E-5 (Sgt)
- Attended Loyola University. Obtained MS in Counseling Psych in 1/79. Moved to California 12/79
- Worked private practice as Vocational Psychologist 09/80-11/96.
- Returned to school - National University - MA Special Education. Two teaching credentials (Multiple Subject K-12 and Special Education, Mild/Moderate). Taught Special Education grades 9-12 from 1996-2016. Also coached cross country, wrestling and other sports.
- Managed to obtain my Ph.D. In Metaphysical Theology in 1999.
- Married 4 times. Two sons, both RN's (Grant and Josh).
- Enjoys playing guitar and riding motorcycles

This Belongs to Bryan MacKay '73, Biological Sciences

MiniMester on the Battlefield

In the early days of UMBC, MiniMester was a full four weeks long, encompassing the entire month of January. Many of us felt it was a great opportunity to take courses of interest, rather than those required for a major. Professors felt the same way. One such course in January 1970 was "Military History of the Civil War", taught by the popular teacher and well-known historian James Mohr. A major attraction was four all-day bus trips to several snowy, frozen battlefields in Virginia, Maryland and Pennsylvania.

But the first hurdle was to get into the course. Everyone I knew wanted to take it. Registration was entirely first come, first served, irrespective of major or number of credits earned. So long before dawn on a frigid winter morning, I took my place in line outside the old Hillcrest building, then home to the Registrar's office. Every single person ahead of me was there to register for this course, but fortunately I was number 21 in line for a course with a maximum enrollment of 40 (the capacity of the bus).

The course was everything I hoped it would be. I learned a lot, and Dr. Mohr was a great teacher. He was a superb lecturer, but friendly and approachable. All of us loved him. On the bus trip to Antietam, Dr. Mohr brought a metal detector. He explained that although it was illegal to use the metal detector on federally-owned national battlefields, we would be stopping at a site atop the Blue Ridge that saw a nasty little fight in 1862, and was still in private hands, where we could look for old spent minie balls, belt buckles, and other accoutrements.

At the Antietam visitor center and store, one wag bought a replica Civil War bullet. Later, as we trooped off the bus into slush and mud and a frigid wind, the student walked ahead of Dr. Mohr, dropped the bullet, and ground it into the soil with his boot. Immediately thereafter, Dr. Mohr's metal detector began clicking wildly, to the utter amazement of our professor. Dr. Mohr found the bullet; he was so excited! Only when we were back on the bus did the student come clean and confess; all of us, including Dr. Mohr, had a good laugh about it.

I enjoyed many of my courses at UMBC, but Military History of the Civil War was my favorite.

After UMBC:

- Received MS, UMBC 1979
- Worked for 33 years at UMBC as instructor, lecturer, senior lecturer; retired 2012

- Published 5 books (with Johns Hopkins University Press) on nature and outdoor activities in Maryland
- Married Debi Sandford in 2003; we met on a hiking trip in Scotland
- I've never lived, worked or gone to school outside Catonsville
- I do occasionally leave the zip code for vacation, having been to 49 states and all the National Parks in the lower 48

Dr. James Mohr, History, and Students on the Battlefield

This Belongs to Sal Maggio '72, Psychology

Gimme Shelter!

I attended UMBC from 1968-1972 and was always proud to be part of the founding years of a university that has continued to expand and develop their academic reputation. Below are some of my fondest memories:

I served as Vice President of Student Government during my junior year. My most memorable event (and fun story) that I still tell my friends relates to an event where Senator Fulbright was invited to speak at the university as part of our Speaker Series. I had the privilege of sitting next to him at lunch, but while I was holding a conversation with another person, Senator Fulbright got up to leave and I realized I hadn't yet thanked him. I jumped up and ran after him, however I soon found that my feet were no longer touching the ground since two Secret Service agents had deterred me from reaching the senator! With an "OK" from the senator, they put me back down and I was able to offer a gracious farewell (although a little less dignified than I had planned!)

UMBC was founded during a time of unrest on many college campuses, often fueled by protests of the Vietnam War. I remember staying overnight in a campus building as part of a nonviolent protest. At the time, Bill Soltesz was President of Student Government and asked for us to help keep order. In hindsight I'm not sure we were capable of that high task. Still, I remember the Security Guards were very respectful toward us and the event served as effective protest without major upset.

I remember that student orientation took place at the Donaldson Brown Center in Port Deposit. The women stayed in a large mansion (likely owned by the university) and the guys slept in converted stables (but they were still very nice).

UMBC was still under construction in those early years and there was mud everywhere. I remember receiving a parking ticket for parking in a faculty space. I took a picture of the messy parking space and was successfully able to defend myself in student court that this space was in fact unrecognizable as faculty parking.

Two very popular faculty from that era were Marty Schwartz (a plaque honoring Marty's service is located outside of the Biology building) and Dr. Robert Burchard. Both professors were known for their engagement with students. Marty had breakfast with me on numerous occasions and we got to know each other pretty well. Marty was head of the Biology Department and kept a greenhouse. He was very dedicated to developing an academically competitive department.

He talked about wanting to assure that a degree in Biology from UMBC would allow students admittance to medical school. Dr. Burchard was also a biology professor who spent plenty of time talking with students about issues relevant to them; he was also active in political meetings such as the New Democratic Coalition. He was very well liked and trusted by students.

My best accomplishment as part of UMBC student government was to have a bus stop shelter installed so students would not have to stand in the rain. I still live near UMBC and my wife and I take walks around the campus. I always point out the bus shelter to her. The truth is, I'm not really sure it's the same shelter I ordered but it makes me feel good!

After UMBC:

- Received a Master's Degree from Loyola University.
- Worked for Anne Arundel County Schools as a teacher and administrator for 40 years.
- Traveled to Italy, England, France, Germany, Austria, Norway, Sweden, Denmark, Canada and Slovakia.
- Married with 4 children and 8 grandchildren.
- Currently lives in Catonsville.

Going to the New Bus Shelter

This Belongs to Nancy Frey Malloy '70, Biological Sciences

UMBC's First State Certified Biology Teacher

I really enjoyed reading my classmates' stories about their experiences at the beginning of UMBC. They brought back many great memories as well as the feeling of how special it was for us to have had that time together. One common thread that we all had, I think can be found in the word "opportunity". It was such an amazing thing to be part of the beginning of a new university. How many people get to do that? I always felt extremely lucky and blessed to be one of the members of the original class at UMBC. I never took it for granted, and always felt a sense of adventure as each new experience unfolded.

Like some of my classmates, many of my opportunities came about because of being able to work at UMBC. In the beginning, there were only a few science research labs. Biology, Chemistry, and Physics researchers were neighbors in the basement of the (only) Academic Building. As new professors came on board, some had very limited resources and that included a lack of lab assistants. Dr. Walt Konetzka, Science Department Chair, had enough status and grant resources to have an actual lab technician. Such was not immediately the case for Dr. Neil Mendelson who came to work in the same lab. Hence, one of my most special opportunities came as an invitation to work in their lab as an assistant during my freshman year. I was fortunate to have Vaughn Crouch as my mentor. She was Dr. Konetzka's technician and I learned so much from her. Because we were working in a microbiology research lab, sterile technique was paramount. However, it's important to note that back in the beginning that meant making your own agar broth and pouring it into petri dishes with great care. These were glass dishes. And in the less glamorous part of my $1.25/hr. job, I washed those dishes as well as test tubes. It was quite a thrill when a dishwasher was installed. Sterilization didn't always involve the use of an autoclave. We had a fairly small one, which I recall was out of order for a period of time. Resources were expanded by the use of good old-fashioned pressure cookers. I have a vivid memory of Dr. Bob Burchard rushing into the hallway and colliding with me as he attempted to get away from a possible explosion. Fortunately, he had been able to vent enough steam out to prevent a disaster.

When Dr. Mendelson was able to hire an actual lab technician, I was fortunate to be kept on as a stockroom assistant and worked for the inimitable Mr. Phil Martin. As UMBC's science department grew, the need for different equipment and supplies did as well. Our metal shelves, which I had been taught to assemble, became more and more full. We didn't have computers to compile a running inventory, it was all handwritten, and kept in a kind of card catalog. We were constantly behind in "posting" – transcribing from the little slips of paper where people wrote down what was taken from the stockroom. And if we didn't have what someone needed, Phil could usually cobble something together for them in the meantime. It was quite the operation.

As much as I loved my job, an opportunity came about in my Senior Year that lured me away, although not very far. It occurred to the faculty that with their ever-growing student enrollment they could really use some teaching assistants. But T.A.'s are normally graduate students, and UMBC still didn't have those. They just had us, and we would have to do. So, I was offered a job as a biology lab T.A. By that time, I had decided on teaching as my career path and along with my major I was taking education courses so that I could be certified as a high school teacher. What a tremendous opportunity it was to work in the environment of freshman biology and be confident that teaching was something I would love doing after graduation. (I eventually became UMBC's first state certified biology teacher.)

During my first year of teaching, I began to take a graduate education course at College Park. But between the stress of being a first-year teacher, the long commute, and my heart not really being in it, I withdrew. Around that time, UMBC announced that they would begin a Master's Degree program in Biology. Again, a wonderful opportunity was being offered. I applied, but admission was not a slam dunk. Although there were professors who knew me and the quality of my work, there was one professor who opposed my admission. He didn't know me, but was opposed on principle to having part-time graduate students. He was of the opinion that one had to be devoted full time to study and research in order to be a graduate student in the field. Fortunately for me, there was enough support from the other faculty for the notion that if you give a first-class graduate education to a teacher, she could better educate her own students. I was able to take my classes in the evening and do research in the summers in the labs of Dr. Burchard and Dr. Brian Bradley. I received my M.S. in Biological Sciences in 1975 in the field house (not yet called the RAC), which was built after our first graduation that had taken place on the lawn. I was proud to send some of my best students on to UMBC where they had the opportunity to major in biology and go on to become doctors and other members of the health care professions. It all came around full circle.

It was such a privilege to be one of the first students and take part in many "firsts" at UMBC. I will forever be grateful for every opportunity I was given, for the outstanding teachers and staff, and for my wonderful classmates and friends.

After UMBC:

- Received M.S. UMBC 1975, as one of the first UMBC graduate students
- Taught Biology at Atholton High School 1970-1978
- Worked at Our Lady of Perpetual Help School 1990-2011: Taught K-8 Computer, Asst. Principal 1996-2001, Principal 2001-2011
- Worked at St. Augustine School 2011-2017: Registrar/Student records manager 2011-2016, Acting Principal 2016-2017
- Married Mike Malloy in 1974
- Mom of Kate, UMBC 1999, and Kevin, UMBC 2005; Grandmother of twins Madison and Mason
- Retired and enjoying life with Mike in Ellicott City

UMBC Student Teachers

This Belongs to Robin Keller Mayne '70*, American Studies

The First Graduate

I arrived at UMBC in September of 1966, bringing with me two years of evening class credits from University College in downtown Baltimore. As I looked around at the incoming freshmen, I felt so "old" even though I was only 2 years ahead of my classmates. My situation was quite a bit more complicated than the typical student: I had a darling, 2-year old daughter at home so I knew I would be having to juggle competing priorities to complete my degree. But I loved this new opportunity which presented itself to me and enthusiastically looked forward to once again becoming a part of a community of students seeking education.

I remember the excitement (and some confusion) of walking into registration and seeing all the departmental tables set up. It reminded me of a tag-team sport in which students attempted to "nab" as many of the flags (i.e., IBM course cards) as they could get to fill out their proposed semester schedule. The cards listed the department, course and section number and a student count number (the total number of students allowed in that section).

Of course, in the first year, nearly everyone was a freshman. Everyone moved as quickly as possible to secure what they needed to make their schedule work, before courses began to close. After gathering all your cards, you then took them to a final check-out table where your bill was computed and payment made. You then limped weakly over to the bookstore and began assembling a pile of books for the courses you would be taking. The first hurdle of the semester had been successfully surmounted!

Because of my "advanced age" and responsibilities, I was never able to fully enjoy the usual college activities: clubs, athletics, concerts and dances. There simply weren't enough hours in the day to attend classes, do homework and handle a child in the evening/weekend hours. But I soon added a new responsibility which, surprisingly, really helped me feel a part of this new educational institution.

I took a student assistant position in one of the Academic Divisional Offices. At that time, the Humanities Division and the Social Sciences Divisions were housed on the top floor of the academic building. I began working for the Social Sciences Group and came to feel a real kinship with "my faculty":

Dr. David Lewis (Sociology) – chair
Dr. Frank Burd (Political Science)
Dr. Janice Goldberg (Psychology)

Dr. Augustus Low (History)
Dr. Donald Milsten (Political Science)
Dr. Aristeides Papadakis (History)
Dr. Charles F. Peake (Geography)
Dr. Fred Pincus (Sociology)
Dr. William Rothstein (Sociology)
Dr. Rudolph Storch (History, Classics)

This position gave me a home base on campus and allowed me to get to know faculty outside of class when they could be more approachable and supportive without the rigors of classroom etiquette.

The division secretaries shared an open space with offices on both sides, next to the windows. A counter on top of file cabinets gave further definition to the work environment. The chairs of these divisions (Dr. Robert Shedd - Humanities and Dr. David Lewis -Social Sciences) officed adjacent to the open bull pen. Two long halls of faculty offices led away from the secretarial pool towards the elevators, with Humanities' faculty along the northwest hall and the Social Sciences' faculty on the southeast hall.

Mrs. Smith was the Humanities' secretary but it is Mrs. Fannie Kerpelman (the Social Sciences' secretary) for whom I worked who really sticks out in my mind. She was a wonderfully colorful "mother" figure to all the student helpers and supervised us with loving care. As I recall she had a number of children so she definitely knew how to handle kids (I believe one of her children became a lawyer and served in Baltimore city government). It seemed to me that she wore brightly-colored scarves and her ears were frequently adorned with sparkly, dangle earrings. She was unfailingly optimistic and friendly to everyone she came in contact with.

My typical duties were running errands (take this to so-and-so) and typing syllabi/hand-outs and filing. Of course, typing exams were under Mrs. Kerpelman's exclusive purview since they represented a student version of "classified" material. Back in the day, duplication was done on a mimeograph machine (xeroxing was too expensive) and the master had to be typed on a special form which "cut" into the purple inked back sheet (much like carbon paper). Invariably, the purple ink got everywhere and because Mrs. Kerpelman did so many of these documents, her fingers seemed always tinged with purple.

These two divisions remained housed on that floor for two years, I believe, before faculty growth exceeded the space. Social Sciences was then relocated (some said banished) to the Gray House, across the field to the east. I believe this building was probably the last remaining structure from the farm estate upon which UMBC was built. But I LOVED this old house! I would arrive early on campus (my ride had an 8:00 class) and walked from the parking lot over the field to the Gray House. Frequently, the mist was still "on the moor" and deer could be spotted crossing the meadow and heading for the woods. It's hard to express how idyllic this scene is in my mind. I would often get to the office before anyone else and start the coffee. A TA who came from College Park to teach a survey section would frequently be at a temp desk, going over their notes and anxiously awaiting some bracing brew to wake him up.

Slowly, the building would fill up as Mrs. Kerpelman and the faculty arrived and headed to their respective corners of the house. Quickly, the house would begin "bustling" with activity as faculty picked up handouts and headed across campus to teach. At the 50th anniversary celebration, I had an opportunity to visit with Dr. Rothstein and he recalled how you had to go through his office in the Gray House to get to the bathroom. Primitive doesn't begin to describe the office space but, through it all, I can't remember any real rancor or unpleasantness amongst the faculty (of course, they may have shielded a lowly student from unprofessional behavior). I just remember the feeling of excitement on the part of the faculty that they were a part of something new and different and that feeling was definitely communicated to the student body every day in the classroom.

I am forever grateful to have experienced how really exciting education can be when your professors love what they do and can't wait to share it with their students. And working within an academic division gave me a special insight into those young faculty who were just beginning to carve out their own academic careers as they crafted a new university.

After UMBC:

- Received MSDD (Master of Software Design and Development), TCU 1992
- Worked for Head Start, Financial Investments, Information Technology and Purchasing
- Married 1985 to Jim Mayne. Two children: Cassandra (1964) who frequently visited UMBC and Nicole (deceased 2015), adopted from Korea. One granddaughter, four great-grandsons.
- Lives in Fort Worth, TX near daughter Cassandra.
- "UMBC helped me develop critical thinking skills allowing me to adapt to a number of different fields throughout my professional career."

*Robin actually completed her degree requirements in 1969, but there was no Commencement until June 1970.

This Belongs to Charles S. McCubbin, Jr. '73, History

Local Boy

Quite literally I was a Founding Four before there was even a UMBC. You see I went to Arbutus Junior High directly across Shelbourne Road from the old Spring Grove State Hospital farm. When I had classes in the front of the building you could watch the patients at the hospital working in the fields. The state mental health hospitals and other facilities had to be self-sustaining in those days, and Spring Grove had been carved out of one of the big original Catonsville area estates. Just as my junior high school, Catonsville High School and later on Catonsville Community College.

I had English, Science and Spanish in those front classrooms and watched the workers caring for vegetables and fruits growing in the fields directly across the road. We were often warned by faculty and staff not to interact with the farm workers. In the summer, when the windows were open, you could smell the peach blossoms from the farm.

While I was at Catonsville High, UMBC was just beginning. By this time the old farm was gone and many of the original buildings were going up at UMBC. I had a friend in some of my high school classes and I would often give him a ride home. He lived in this big mansion on the hill overlooking the growing campus. His name was Albin O. Kuhn II and his father was the first Chancellor of the UMBC campus. I never really connected with that at the time. I often envied him living in that historical place. We became occasional friends.

I took a gap year, or two, and then attended Catonsville Community College before transferring to UMBC. At that time UMBC was known then as a commuter college, so I lived off campus in Arbutus, and worked to pay for schooling. If I remember the cost of a semester was between $600 and $800 plus books, and fees.

I had to work to pay for schooling I did not get to socialize as much as many of the few residents who did live on campus. The only time I socialized was between classes and doing research in the library. I was serious about my schooling, and I never was much of a social butterfly anyway.

You had to spend an additional $15 for a parking permit. When I was in my last semester I bought a new car, had perhaps a month until graduation so the campus police let me slide on a new (additional $15) parking sticker. At the end there were so many new buildings, and so many new students that you had to park on the hill, near the Wilkens Avenue police station and walk down. I remember that it was cold in the winter and hot in the summer as we walked through construction projects that were going up. Wooden sidewalks were somewhat of a luxury and it was always an adventure when they put new fences up right where and when you had a short cut.

During my first semester I took a class on World War II. It was my introduction to large lecture halls and it was imposing. I felt small and had absolutely no idea what was going on initially. But I muddled through class and life went on. It was the only large lecture class I took.

During the first winter session in January I took a chess class from my French history professor. I remember that we had to play a chess game using gambits and defenses we had learned. One of the other students was a returning Vietnam Vet. Many of the other students were anti-war and would have nothing to do with him and would not play with him. I quickly learned that as a vet he had been trained to do what the military does best, be aggressive. He was a most aggressive and logical player. I never won a game from him, but I learned a lot.

I took a class in early Christian History, it covered the late Roman Empire through the Early Middle Ages. The professor had a strange sense of humor, and he often showed it in some very strange ways. For the first exam he came into the class just in time and turning his back to the class wrote on the blackboard "Nos morituri te salutamus "or "We who are about to die salute you". He explained that this was the salute of the gladiators in the coliseum and generally pertained to students who academically die after a test.

My major was history specifically European history. In that final semester the Bachelor Thesis Seminar was taught by the professor who had a specialty in Renaissance history. The second class session he handed out assignments and I got the topic *Military Institutions of Anglo-Saxons Prior to the Norman Invasion of 1066*. Which is only good for discussing the fine points of Medieval English society whilst standing in the unemployment line. No joke, that's all it's good for!
I wish I had kept a copy of my thesis, and I always planned to go back to the main library and see if they had a copy, but business kept me traveling around and time, as it always does, passed on.

Graduation ceremonies were held outdoors the year I graduated. The speaker was B. F. Skinner. Since I had vigorously avoided the hard sciences much of it was over my head. But I made it through it and walked the aisle to get the rolled up scroll that said I could have my diploma after I turned in my cap and gown. My diploma did not say UMBC or University of Maryland Baltimore County because the school was not yet accredited. It said University of Maryland, but after 6 years of blood, sweat, and tears I was just as happy and just as proud.

I had two choices for employment after graduation: sell men's suits at a Robert Hall store. Or I could go to work at USF&G as an underwriter. I chose USF&G.

While I did go on to graduate school and earn a Master's in Business Administration it was the discipline of study, school and work that I picked up at UMBC that made me successful in business and in life generally. It was the discipline of research for that useless thesis topic that helped me get my MBA, and finish training for an IT Network Certification later.

No socializing, lots of work, a few good friends. I was just back through the school in the fall of 2021 and felt old and small. The campus with lots of open spaces and scenery seems now to be a mass of buildings, a city jungle in its own right. Our, my, UMBC is gone and in its place is the University of Maryland Baltimore County. A full-fledged University in its own right.

After UMBC:

- Received MBA, University of Baltimore (Management, Finance and Marketing (1976)
- Adjunct Instructor at several Community Colleges and Universities, and Technical Schools
- Senior Project Manager and Team Leader for major Information Technology deployments (1985-2010)
- Published Articles for American Journal of Small Business and U.S. Small Business Administration
- Semi-professional photographer in Landscape, Glamour and Fashion

Park Where You Can Find Some Space

This Belongs to Thornton (Mack) McIver '72, Economics

My Top Ten Memories

The first ten things I remembered as I started this project. These items are in no particular order and remember these recollections are about events occurring around 55 years ago.

10. My first day on campus (a late summer humid day of Baltimore weather +90 degrees). This freshman wore a sport coat and necktie. Yes! A sports coat. I DIDN'T DO THAT AGAIN!!!

9. Trips up and down the steep hill to the Hillcrest admissions office. At least twice that day in an attempt to get my schedule right. Yes! Still in a sport coat and tie.

8. The number of dormitories that had been constructed by1967. (The answer will be revealed soon.)

7. Not many buildings were constructed at this time. Let me see if I can name them. The academic building, bookstore/student union, the multi-purpose building, the cafeteria, the lecture hall…and of course, the library with Mr. Gillespie and Mr. Wiegarde at the security desk.

6. Oops! There was also a Plant housing the Maintenance and security staff.

5. Some, but not all, of the professors and staff that I interacted with were as follows: Dr. Peake, Chairman of the Economics Dept. Mr. Rawlings, Math Instructor, who later became a delegate in the Md. state legislature; Dr. Klein, professor of history (Western Civilization); Dr. Ernest Murphy, professor of International Economics; Dr. Marsha Goldfarb, also an economics professor; Mr. Watts, the athletic Director and Lacrosse coach; Dr. Aziz, professor of Mathematics (Calculus); Dr. Sadie Fletcher, Guidance Counselor and last but certainly not least, Dr. Betty Glascoe, the director of Career Development and Job Placement.

4. The number of students attending UMBC during the 1967-68. I don't know the exact number but I am sure it was somewhere around 600. YES! 600, give or take a 100.

3. When "MiniMester" started (the 4 week winter session) I remember taking a course using IBM 12 row/80-column punched card format which came to dominate the industry as a primary medium for input of both computer programs and data. As of 2012 these cards are now obsolete as a storage medium. Now it is important to remember that this "ERA" was pre everything.

A.) pre electric typewriter

B.) pre cell phones

C.) pre wireless home phone sets

D.) pre laptops

E.) and WAY-Y-Y-Y-Y-Y-Y BEFORE THE INTERNET …ETC., ETC., ETC.

2.   OOPS! I almost forgot. The answer to the 8th top ten memory is ZERO (0). There were no dorms on campus during the 1967-1968 period.

Thunder Thornton

1.   Last but not least, one of my best memories occurred during the Intramural basketball season when "yours truly" got a write-up in the retriever newspaper for scoring 27 points in victory. Additionally, the author of the article nicknamed me "THUNDER THORNTON". Unfortunately, that season was my first and last intramural basketball competition.

 Foot note*. About 10 years ago I tried to retrieve a copy of the article, but apparently the Retriever archives do not have records that far back.

After UMBC:

- 1972-1977 Worked at UMBC in The Student Services Learning Resources Program
- 1977-2006: Worked in private industry in various human resources and operations positions. Won the Eagle Award in 1984. This is an annual award given to the most outstanding employee in our division.
- Retired (HALELUJAH!) 2006 – Present: Volunteer work at My Sister's Place (assisted in feeding the homeless); participated as a facilitator in the Leadership Development Institute; at our Church from 2017-2020; and more recently (2021 to present) assist in teaching and enhancing a recurring Personal Finance Course entitled, "Where Is Your Money?", coaching participants on managing their financial matters.
- July 21, 1973: Married my college sweetheart, Towanda Shaw, also a UMBC graduate in Economics. Live in Turf Valley Overlook and love to travel

Making New Friends on the First Day of Classes

This Belongs to Mindy R. Milstein '72, Psychology

Psyched Out

I had gone to American University in Washington DC with a plan to study journalism. When I took Psychology 101, I fell in love with Psychology and changed my major. Unfortunately, the program was very narrow due to a department head that only believed in a narrow theory of psychology. I knew a few people from my graduating class and the classes of '67 and '66 from Milford Mill HS who had gone to UMBC. I decided to transfer.

At UMBC, the psychology department was awesome right out of the gate. My advisor Jonathan Finkelstein was inspiring and ultimately helped me get my PhD at UMBC 17 years later. Aaron Seigman was challenging and hired me as a teaching assistant so that I could pay for my doctorate. There were many top psychology professors that prepared me well for a lifelong career in the field.

Beyond psychology, there were English teachers that inspired me to love Shakespeare and Philosophy professors who taught me how to make logical arguments. I loved it!

In fact, I loved it so much that both my son (class of 1996) and my daughter (class of 2000) went to UMBC on Humanities Scholarships and I earned a PhD in Clinical Psychology in 1997. Dr. Hrabowski wrote the reference for law school for both of my kids.

After UMBC:

- Completed my PhD in Psychology UMBC
- "UMBC gave me a great background in Psychology"

Listening to Speakers in Gym One

This Belongs to Paula Heard Moulds '73, History

1 – 2 – 3 – 4

"ONE away"

I spent my first year of college at Florence State University in Alabama (now UNA) while living with my brother Jack. Even though it was a great experience of learning and meeting new people, I became homesick for my family and friends in Maryland.

"SECOND year"

I came to UMBC for my Sophomore year. I took **2** fields of study: Elementary Education and History that would earn me a Bachelor of Arts Degree in 1973. The Education classes were marvelous because I've always wanted to become a teacher. The History classes were more challenging, mostly to keep up with the reading assignments. U.S. History was my favorite under the leadership of Dr. Low.

"THREE bears"

UMBC campus was like *The Three Bears* story...not too big, not too small, but just right for me! I've always been a commuter, so I headed from home on I-695 (usually amid some heavy traffic) to attend my weekday classes.

"Another FOUR to follow"

My son, Clint Moulds IV, chose UMBC for his Bachelor of Science in Computer Science in 1998. Like me he commuted from home, but it was much easier due to the opening of I-195. After receiving several scholarships, he was one of the few students who earned money by going to college.

In closing, I'm a History major who made history at UMBC. I'm honored to be part of their Founding Four Alumni!

After UMBC:

- Career of 30 years as a substitute teacher in A.A. County Public Elementary Schools.
- Married Clint Moulds III in 1973.
- Two sons (Clint IV and Steve) and one grandson (Victor).
- Retired and living in Millersville, MD.

This Belongs to Jack Mullen '72, Economics

Zero to Hero

I consider my UMBC experience to be so transformational for me that it probably changed my life trajectory from one that was meant to be somewhat mundane to one that has been truly extraordinary. I often find my own story after I graduated from UMBC to be almost unbelievable, but am reassured it was real based on all the pictures, articles and other memorabilia that I accumulated over the 50 years since I graduated. So…. What was so special about going to UMBC that changed my life trajectory? I remember the line from "Titanic" in which Kate Winslet's character says her experience with Leonardo DiCaprio's character "saved her in every way she could be saved". This what happened to me at UMBC.

The first thing special about UMBC was that I had never gone to school with such friendly students, faculty and staff. Their friendliness to me made the experience feel like 4 years in Disneyland. I was an Army brat and grew up going to 16 different schools by the time I finished formal education. Only at UMBC did I feel like I was treated like a human being rather than a number to be run through the system. I attended Mt St Joseph High school before UMBC and it was like going to work in a salt mine everyday rather than the "Disneyland" I experienced at UMBC. Like the song from Cheers, I felt that everybody at UMBC "knew my name" in contrast to nobody but my home room classmates at Mt St Joe. I still cannot understand how two school experiences could be so different but I think it's because at St Joe we were treated like children and part of a systematic production line, but at UMBC we were treated like adults and like special guests (hence UMBC felt like a vacation in "Disneyland" in comparison).

For example, Mr. Watts, UMBC's Athletic Director, knew my name very quickly and was very friendly toward me and it was probably because I was on UMBC's basketball team and our home games were in gym that was central to student life on campus. I also made UMBC's baseball team which probably enlarged my circle of friends and made me even more well-known among coaches and students. This type of friendly treatment extended to Mr. Woolston, the registrar, who played basketball in the gym, Mr. Libby, Director of Student Life, and all the teachers who played pickup basketball in the gym such as Dr. Sherwin, Dr. Storch, and Dr. Joel Jones, and Dr. Taylor (economics).

Whenever I had a class with one if these professors, they recognized me in class and this made me work harder to get a good grade because I did not want to look dumb in their subject. As a result, I received two A's and a B in the three courses

I had with them. FYI, I was much more interested in sports at UMBC than studying and so I had all C's and one D in my regular courses in my Freshman year along with an A in my MiniMester course which was only a 1 or 2 credit course. As a result, I ended with a 1.8 GPA and was on probation.

My desire to continue at UMBC was so strong that it caused me to take studying much more seriously in my later years and my grades improved so much that I even had a GPA of 3.5 in the Spring semester of my Junior year and graduated with a 2.7 overall and a 3.2 in Economics. I credit the personal rapport I developed with these professors, the coaches and the staff that I dealt with at UMBC with my transformation into a serious student from someone who loved sports and had a hard time studying. This trend continued after I graduated from UMBC when I earned an MBA at Loyola College with a GPA of 3.5 and ranked 3rd in the class on the comprehensive exam we had to take to graduate.

The other aspect about UMBC that was transformational was my ability to actually achieve my goals as opposed to my inability to do this at Mt St Joe. For example, I was cut from the baseball team at St Joe despite the fact that I was a decent player and I was third string on the varsity football team for two years and was never put in a game. In contrast, I had the opposite experience at UMBC and made the varsity basketball and baseball teams and saw enough playing time to earn a letter in each sport for each year that I played. In addition, I actually played well enough in intercollegiate competition that I contributed directly to wins against Johns Hopkins and University of Baltimore in basketball and Towson State in baseball. This gave me a positive attitude about the ability to successfully achieve my goals and succeed in my education. These twin accomplishments gave me a "can do attitude" toward my future goals in business that enabled me to rank in the top three people in my profession as a derivatives sales leader on Wall St.

During my 28 year career on "Wall Street" I became an industry leader in derivatives and led successful derivative sales teams for Chase Manhattan Bank, Citibank, First Chicago, Security Pacific Bank (now Bank of America), and was Director of Derivatives for the Farm Credit Bank in MN, and to do these jobs I lived in LA, Chicago, St Paul, NYC, and London. After these jobs, I was recruited to join the Board of Directors of Bank OZK, which was ranked the 7th best and biggest construction lender in the US. In closing, I credit my entire career path as described above to the transformational experience that I had at UMBC, that taught me that I could achieve almost anything if I worked hard enough and treated others the way I was treated at UMBC. UMBC left me with a golden rule for my career that I would never try to get ahead at the expense of someone else and so I avoided the typical backstabbing that generally comes with jobs on Wall Street because it's so competitive. Hey, I always thought that if I could score the tying point against Hopkins a minute before the win, the winning run against Towson State in the last inning and get an A in Microeconomics at UMBC, then I could do almost anything I put my mind to.

One last thing is that I also enjoyed the friendly treatment I received from all the students I encountered at UMBC and want to thank all of you for this kind behavior. This great experience with fellow students was also transformational for me because I had not been to a school in which so many students I met were nice to me. This helped form my golden rule for treating others for the rest of my life. In fact, I am still in touch with Bill Wade and Rich Hammock from the Basketball team and Louie Sowers who is in UMBC's sports Hall of Fame for Women's sports. We traded emails of astonishment and congratulations when UMBC beat number 1 seeded Virginia in the NCAA basketball tournament a few years ago and continue to email each other from time to time.

UMBC…Thanks for the Memories….

I have too many great memories of my years at UMBC to list them in a short story, but the ones that come to mind the most frequently are related to sports, the engaging faculty and staff and a few of the extracurricular activities.

My favorite basketball memory was scoring the tying basket in a come from behind win against Johns Hopkins in my freshmen year and for the first time in my life I heard a large cheer from our intrepid fans in the stands as the ball went through the basket. Thanks to steady scoring from Bruce Kent and Richard (Gus) Hammock throughout the game, we pulled ahead in the final minutes and won the game.

My favorite baseball memories were scoring the winning run in the top of the last inning against Towson State and being carried off home plate by my teammates, and we held the lead and won the game. And the best ... I hit a stand up triple with bases loaded against the Military Academy Prep School and while standing on third base I heard a lacrosse player who had run over to the baseball field to see what all the noise was about and then yell over to the lacrosse field in a loud voice I could hear while standing on third base, "Jack Mullen hit a triple with bases loaded" which implied that the lacrosse players even knew who I was. This memory made my day and still gives me a smile whenever I need one.

At this point I would like to express my gratitude for many fond memories of UMBC to the coaches, staff and my fellow teammates: Coaches and staff include, John Frank (basketball) and Tom Rider (baseball), Louie Lyall Sowers our basketball team scorekeeper, AD Dick Watts and his admin assistant Joanne Bushman, and Mr. Larkin, equipment room manager, who I worked part time for. Fellow teammates whose names I can still remember include Bill Wade, Gus Hammock, Bruce Kent, Tyrone Joyner, Clyde Emerson Small, Glen Begly, Steve Masgay, and Craig O'Connell from the Basketball Team, and Tom Hughes, Mike Hoban, Ed Sherman, Tom Myers, Wally Islam, Fritz Lahner, Paul Kopeck, and Rich Sorocoe from the Baseball Team. I also want to thank our amazing cheerleading team and the few members I can remember like Linda Dunn, Nancy Campbell and Betty Tittsworth. They were excellent cheerleaders and always gave us a much needed emotional lift when they cheered for the UMBC teams.

I also have great memories of watching the various women's sports teams play basketball, volleyball and field hockey, and their cast of outstanding players that I can remember included Frannie Daum, Barbie and Pat Callan, Julie Tuminelli, and Louie Lyall Sowers who seemed to play on every team and were good enough to finish 7th in the State in Basketball.

Finally, I have great memories of playing basketball in the gym with faculty and staff members like Dr. Jones, Dr. Sherwin and Mr. Woolston who were good players and were fun to play with along with fellow students who played frequently in the gym like I did. I still remember yelling at Dr. Jones, Dr. Sherwin and Mr. Woolston across the basketball court to let them know when I was open for a pass and I enjoyed playing basketball with fellow students like Bobby and Jimmy Zepp, Skip Carroll, Roy Walker, Willie Lehrer, Glen Smink, Bob Wobbeking, and the other students who frequented the gym like I did. I know I would have earned much better grades if UMBC did not have the gym open for student play every day. The open gym was like cheese to a mouse to me and I could not resist going in to play every chance I had.

The extracurricular activities at UMBC were also great and the ones that stand out were: Casino night, movie night in the Lecture Hall, the scavenger Hunt, the outdoor sports, barbecue and bonfire day, the Halloween costume dance and the other mixers, and the theater group putting on great plays with UMBC's top acting talent. I also have an enduring memory of watching Nancy Campbell sing "Both Sides Now" in 1967 in the Student Union Building as well as Joni Mitchell did at a talent show that I happened upon between classes and I still play this song to revive the cool memory of that day at UMBC.

In closing, if you ever watched the great classic movie "Citizen Kane", then you will understand when I say that my time at UMBC will always be my version of "Rosebud". The self-confidence, the caring environment, the high ethical standard, and the solid education I gained in Economics and English enabled me to rise to the very top of my field in derivatives on Wall Street and motivated me to give part of my financial success back to UMBC primarily in the form of specially designated endowments in honor of Dr. Sherwin (Ancient Studies), Mr. Woolston (UMBC Registrar), Gary Rupert (Alumni affairs), and Dr. Peake (Economics) which have a market value today of over $250,000. I established these endowments so they could grow over time to enable future generations to reap benefits.

I would like to offer a final group of thank yous to Freeman Hrabowski for providing outstanding leadership for UMBC for more than 25 years, and more recently to Cheryll Ratzsch and to UMBC Founding Four alums Diane, Mimi and Dale for keeping the Founding Four graduating classes connected to UMBC.

UMBC... Thanks for the memories!

After UMBC:

- Received MBA in Finance from Loyola College in 1974
- Started a 48 year international career in finance that included being a summer teller at First National Bank of Maryland when I was still a UMBC student, followed by Maryland National Bank as a Commercial Banking trainee, and then hired by Commercial Credit Company in Baltimore as the Manager of International Finance and foreign exchange exposures. Worked in banks and financial institutions in derivatives, swaps, hedge funds, and international banking.
- Now self-employed in investments and financial advice.
- UMBC Outstanding Alumni award in 1996. UMBC Outstanding Economics award in 1996
- Married Carol Hardin (UMBC class of '70) in 1973, have 4 children and 5 grandchildren as of 2022.
- Finally…. Many thanks to my classmates, basketball and baseball teammates, as well as the faculty, staff and coaches at UMBC for creating such a wonderful experience for me at UMBC.

UMBC Basketball 1969

This Belongs to Darlene Huggins Murphy '71, American Studies

"Go ahead and Start Them!"

I recently received a phone call from a friend of mine who heard "Sittin' on the Dock of the Bay" by Otis Redding and had to call. We both said (at the very same time): "BEST DANCE EVER!!!". What a trip down memory lane I took. I kept that ticket and decided to look for it. What I found was a treasure trove of souvenirs from our first days at UMBC! I spent over an hour rereading copies of our newspaper. The first copy was dated September 19, 1966 and was called "UMBC News". By November of that same year, it was called "The Retriever". I read each page of issues from September 1966 through March 1968. They are worn and old but the memories they brought back were as fresh as when they happened.

Since our campus was a commuter school, our social lives were important. We were the impetus for every committee and club that formed. Having been a cheerleader in high school, one of the first things I did was talk to Mr. Richard Watts, Athletic Director, about cheerleaders. His comment was, "Go ahead and start them!" Our very first squad consisted of 5 – Nancy Campbell, Donna Helm, Sue Imbach, Betty Tittsworth, and me. We held try-outs and 4 more joined the following year – Carol Apperson, Sherry Cooper, Debbie Wojtczak and Linda Dunn. We did not have too many sports for which we could cheer but we did what we could!

Having worked in the Student Life office entitled me to appear for the very first time on television! WJZ had a Sunday afternoon program called "Newsmakers". Janice Muse, Mark Regan, Al Johnson, and I along with 3 students from Morgan State College questioned Dr. Thurmond Templeton, Executive Director of Baltimore Urban League, concerning race riots. Student Life also entitled me to be one of the sophomores staying at The Donaldson Brown Center for freshman orientation. Nancy Campbell, Wayne Kaiser, Mark Regan, Barbara Scott, Leonard Brown, and I were to give students' perspectives on our institution. We had so much fun, and I hope some insight for the freshman.

I found myself involved with the social committee, the SAGE Players, modern dance, snowball fights, lectures and so many things I cannot remember them all! (I do remember a trip to New York City with Miss Connie Adams to experience Martha Graham and the Peppermint Lounge!).

Our time at UMBC was historical and we are part of a legacy that is hard to duplicate. The memories are priceless, and I thank my friend for starting my trip down memory lane.

PS – My husband still loves to quote my famous line from 'The Male Animal': "Ed – eat your vegetables!"

After UMBC:

- Received a Master's in Curriculum and Instruction - Loyola
- Taught elementary and middle school for 30 years
- Married Norman Murphy, 1970
- Two sons: Shane and Ryan
- One grandson: Nalo
- Retired in 2010 and moved to Ocean Pines

First Newspaper

Rah Rah UMBC

This Belongs to Janice Elizabeth Muse '71, American Studies

Musing through the Good Times

As one of the 700 students in the first class to walk onto the UMBC campus, I have some great memories which come to mind after perusing UMBC early yearbooks almost 56 years later. These memories encompass unique social activities, sporting events, concerts by up-and-coming famous groups, interactions with faculty, and travel experiences during the UMBC MiniMester, now referred to as the Winter Session.

We hustled our way through touch football games on makeshift playing fields. Ahead of our time, we formed coed teams with no hesitation. Down the road, as the campus matured, we turned a campus lake of questionable cleanliness into a battlefield for a tug of war between freshmen and juniors. I participated in a "Miss Student Body" competition and walked away as the winner.

Dancing to the music of Otis Redding shortly before his untimely death, as well as enjoying a concert by a rising group known as Chicago Transit Authority were highlights of our first and second years. We created some unique campus social events such as Casino Night. I manned some of the tables with friend Linda Sugars. Our Halloween dances brought out the costume genius in all of us. During one such celebration, I pushed friend Bob Hinz around in my sister's reinforced makeshift baby carriage.

Making new friends was a daily occurrence and Carol Hesson and Alina Lopez became two of my besties. I even met my husband on campus, but unfortunately, he and the relationship are now a distant memory. I also shared a major crush, with a number of my fellow students, on Dr. Joel Jones, an American Studies professor.

I tried my hand at theatrical performances with the lead in "The Importance of Being Ernest". I also took to modern dance thanks to a class with Connie Wojehowicz. That led to attending a great Martha Graham performance in New York City.

Serious study became a series of adventures with creative faculty. In addition to the usual formal classroom learning, we would travel some weekends to the UMBC-owned Donaldson Brown Center on the bluffs of the Susquehanna River in Port Deposit. There we would have informal discussions with faculty and relax in an atmosphere of splendor and informality. I have memories too of traveling to Civil War battlefields during one MiniMester history course.

My senior year found me working on a senior thesis in American Studies with Dr. Ed Orser on the impact of the new city of Columbia on residents of Howard County. My greatest learning experience, however, was that, with determination, I could successfully graduate even with a learning disability.

After UMBC:

- Worked 30 years as wholesale and retail florist in Roland Park, Ellicott City, and Harborplace
- Worked as life-drawing model (nude) for 15 years.
- Designed Ellicott City Show House for 6 years
- Cleaned houses for 18 years
- Worked as customer service agent with Southwest Airlines, Retired due to COVID
- Still designing flowers for church, parties, funerals and weddings
- Currently involved in Horse rescue
- "UMBC widened my horizons and taught me discipline."
- I thank my pesky fellow grads for convincing me to dig out my UMBC yearbooks and relive the past!

Class Warfare – Tug-O-War

This Belongs to Fran Allen Nickolas '70, American Studies

Number One

My last name was Allen, and my degree was American Studies. That made me "Graduate Number One." As the very first person to walk across the stage, I was nervous and excited at the same time.

More than 50 years later, I admit that I don't remember graduation very clearly. But what I do remember are all of the unique adventures and experiences after that walk across the stage. Thank you, UMBC, for being a stepping stone on the path that became a wonderful life.

Opportunity Knocks

In 1968, I was a student in Dr. Alice Robinson's Oral Interpretation class. Dr. Robinson was not only a fabulous instructor but was also a great person. One day, she approached me and asked if I planned to audition for the Drama Department's production of "Antigone". To be honest, I had never considered it. Dr. Robinson strongly encouraged me to audition. Although I was reluctant, I decided to follow her advice.

The result was being cast as Ismene (Antigone's sister) in the production. I was relieved to know that the part was small - just perfect for my dramatic abilities! Very talented actors and actresses had been cast in the play. I was nervous about my performance. However, this opportunity was a confidence booster, especially when the play concluded!

This whole situation shows that taking a course could result in unexpected and wonderful opportunities. Just a note-the Retriever newspaper clipping, picture, and program were given to me for my 60th birthday by a good friend. She had saved them for many years.

Reflections-Working at the UMBC Student Life Office

One of my most memorable experiences at UMBC was working in the Student Life Office. At that time, the Director was Art Libby. The atmosphere was very congenial. Taking initiative was supported by the staff. As a student, this really helped to build one's confidence.

The responsibilities included conducting tours of the campus for prospective students and working on the student orientation program for incoming students. The orientation program was conducted at the Donaldson Brown Center. Incoming students stayed for a few days at the Center. During this time, students received guidance with course registration and information about the campus activities. In addition to the student orientation staff, members of the UMBC counseling staff were available. The skills developed by working in this environment have lasted a lifetime. All in all, it was a great opportunity for me, and fun as well.

These are personal reflections of an alumni who studied and worked on the UMBC campus from approximately 1966-1970. All I can say is these were wonderful and unforgettable years.

After UMBC:

- Pursued a Master's Degree from University of New Mexico in Albuquerque.
- Married Pete Nickolas (UMBC'71, deceased 2017) and lived on Shaw Air Force Base (South Carolina) with Pete, a Dentist and Captain in the Air Force.
- Moved to Westminster, Maryland and managed family dental practice for 40 years.
- Volunteers for community organizations related to human services, the Arts, and continuing education for seniors.
- Enjoys traveling domestically and internationally, and spending time with her daughter and granddaughter.

New Student Orientation Tour

The Business of UMBC

After having been graduated from the "A" Course at Baltimore City College High School in the spring 1967, I had 30 credits under my belt before even starting UMBC. I had taken calculus in high school. I was late to my first class at UMBC because it was at Hillcrest (administration building) and was in the basement. I was not familiar with the campus layout. When I arrived, the teacher was solving the XYZ equation in broken English. I dropped the course-multivariable calculus. Then, I thought I was taking an easy course in Geology, but that turned out to be quite hard and I dropped that course as well. I majored in Biology. It was actually at the subcellular level. At the time, I lived at home on North Avenue in Baltimore. The dorms at UMBC were not as yet built. Some of the students at UMBC informed me that the initial stood for "U Must Be Crazy," since a good percentage of the initial students failed out. I suspect they felt that it was a fair alternative to Catonsville Community College.

I had a lot of trouble the second semester, since I had to leave home due to the 1968 riots. I was carrying a heavy load at college as well. I did not do well but passed.

The following year, in 1968, I joined the Traffic Court. I do not think we did much and really did not fine anybody. In 1969, I ran unopposed for Treasurer of the SGA. It is there that I made some contacts–Mr. Robert Brown, business manager and Dr. Albin Kuhn, Chancellor, with whom I met regularly to discuss financial matters. I am sure they helped me secure a spot at the University of Maryland, School of Medicine since both of them were transferred from UMBC to the University of Maryland at Baltimore around 1970. (I had a 2.9 GPA.)

While I was Treasurer, I did some foolish things at school, many of which involved other students. In one instance, I remember being carried by 2 other Biology majors through the cafeteria holding a tray with a human brain on it and my head bandaged up as if it had been taken from me. There were some other situations which I cannot repeat. You may run that by some other Biology majors at the time. I remember printing my hand print from the solid ink printing machine all over the SGA office wall. Mr. Art Libby saw it and just shook his head.

Another situation which I regret is not funding the 1970 Skipjack yearbook. I was fairly liberal at the time and used the money ($4000.00) to fund other projects such as a concerts, etc. In that regard, we funded the Chicago Transit Authority to play 2 sets (total of $4000) in 1969, I believe. There was a large crowd at the first concert, but only 100 or so individuals at the second one. They did not want to play the second set but since they were contracted, I called Mr. Brown, business manager and we met with the drummer and they were not happy but played the second set to a small group of students.

After UMBC:

- Briefly attended Graduate School in Biology at UMBC-1970
- Attended Medical School at University of Maryland (1971-1975), then spent a year at Mercy Hospital,
- Worked part time at Johns Hopkins Cytogenetics lab under Dr. Victor Mckusick
- Worked in food services at University of Maryland Hospital in Baltimore
- Residency in Neurology at University of Maryland Hospital (1976-1979)
- Worked in Private Practice in Charlottesville, Virginia (1979-1981)
- Married Anna Gallerizzo, 1978, 3 children and 6 grandchildren
- Moved back to Maryland and has been in Private Practice (in Forest Hill) since 1982
- Lives in Baldwin next to Gunpowder State Park (Sweet Air)

Students Leaving Their Legacy Behind

This Belongs to Marie Pickett '71, American Studies

Awakening a Desire to Learn

Growing up in a home and community in the 1950's and 60's where moms stayed home and the dads were the bread winners, many young women never expected to have a career and schooling was just a way of life. And that was me. But in the late 60's, change was in the air.

For many of us, learning meant earning a passing grade in order to graduate. And one wise professor knew that was true for many of his students. Upon entering his class in the then new 'academic building 2' on the first day of the semester, he instructed us to take out a piece of paper, write our name on it AND the grade we wanted for the course. He collected the papers and announced that the grades for the semester were now out of the way. While I had no idea what others had written, I certainly had put down 'A'. I completed all the assignments for the class but knew I hadn't put forth any real hard work on them. But I got my 'A'!

The next semester I took another course from him. Once again, grades were gotten out of the way on that first day. I put a little more effort into that course but once again, not my best though I began to harbor a little guilt. I finally 'awoke' to real learning by the third class from him and put forth my very best effort and truly believed I earned that 'A'.

While I don't remember his name or the names of the courses, though most likely American literature or American Studies courses, he certainly led me to the realization that I was learning for myself and not a grade. That awakening moment carried over to the rest of my undergrad classes, through grad school, and beyond. What a great, immeasurable gift he gave me that has stayed with me throughout my life!

As things turned out, I wasn't a stay at home wife and mother as I had envisioned; I had a career for 48 years ending with teaching for a local university. I never gave my students that opportunity to self-grade as the courses I taught were specific content driven and my dean would have gone berserk, but I strived to make learning relative, meaningful and enjoyable. Hopefully, to some degree I passed along the love for learning for one's self.

After UMBC:

- Taught for 48 continuous years, Baltimore County elementary and reading specialist

- Taught at University of Notre Dame of Maryland.
- Met my husband at UMBC and our daughter graduated from UMBC in 2021. It will be interesting if her sons will choose UMBC, too.
- "My American Studies professors made college about learning for the betterment of oneself, expanding viewpoints and the desire to never stop learning."

Students Intently Listening in Lecture Hall One

This Belongs to Gene A. Plunka '71, Sociology

Class Act

I enrolled at UMBC as a freshman in fall 1967. I remember an article in the school newspaper that mentioned that the 1967 freshman class consisted of slightly more than nine hundred students. We were the second class to enroll at UMBC, which opened in fall 1966.

Students at UMBC received an excellent education. Many of the faculty were newly minted Ph.D.'s from highly respected schools such as Harvard, Cornell, and Johns Hopkins. They applied high academic standards in the classrooms. Students quickly learned that UMBC was a serious academic environment far from a "party school" (moreover, there were very few social activities in which students could participate). I remember hearing conversations among students who were receiving poor grades and complaining that they were going to transfer to College Park. The attrition rate must have been high because four years later, in June 1971, only 380 students graduated (I still have the1971 UMBC Commencement brochure dated June 6, 1971), and I don't recall any winter or summer graduation ceremonies.

However, like all universities, the teaching was uneven, particularly in upper division courses. In the freshman and sophomore classes, we had the advantage of being taught by Ph.D.'s, unlike other larger state universities where lower division courses were often taught by graduate assistants. When the university grew in those early years, more upper division Instructors were required to teach the majors in junior and senior level courses. I majored in Sociology, and I distinctly recall being taught by Instructors without PhDs who were not the most astute teachers. Eventually, those weak teachers were weeded out of the university.

Registration for courses was archaic, certainly by today's academic standards. Courses were listed on a board, and when classes you wanted were closed, you were left with few choices. I remember that during registration for Spring 1968 classes, one of the few options available was Geography 0200 (Urban Geography) taught by Dr. Starr. So I signed up for the course even though I had no idea what to expect or what I was going to be taught. The course was taught in the large lecture hall, which was almost full to capacity, so apparently a lot of other students who were left with few other options decided to enroll in the course. I actually enjoyed the class and learned a lot about a subject I knew nothing about.

Although I took plenty of social sciences courses and science classes, I enjoyed the humanities classes the most. In my sophomore year, I enrolled in two semesters of a year-long survey of French literature from the Middle Ages to the modern period taught by Dr. Angela Moorjani. Because I was the only person in the class not majoring in French and since I wanted to do well in those classes, I spent a considerable amount of time in the library reading critical literature on the fiction writers, poets, and playwrights that we were studying in class; this library research ultimately was the foundation for the research work that prepared me for graduate study. The following year, I took another useful two-semester course sequence that Dr. Moorjani taught on twentieth-century French literature; during this time period, Dr. Moorjani had completed her dissertation on Samuel Beckett at Johns Hopkins. Dr. Moorjani graciously allowed me to do several Special Project courses with her (similar to Independent Study) on the French theater of the absurd and on the plays and fiction of Samuel Beckett.

My study of French literature was a major influence on my career as a scholar and teacher of modern and contemporary drama. After graduating from UMBC in 1971, I decided not to pursue further study in sociology. Instead, I went to the University of Maryland at College Park, where I earned my M.A. in 1972 and my Ph.D. in 1978—both degrees in comparative literature. My dissertation was on modern drama. Afterwards, I worked for several years as a technical writer and editor at various consulting firms in Rockville and Silver Spring, Maryland. I finally landed a tenure-track position in academia in the Department of English at the University of Memphis in fall 1983. I was promoted to Full Professor there in 1994. I taught at the University of Memphis for 36.5 years and finally retired in December 2019. During my teaching career at the University of Memphis, I published nine scholarly books, fifty academic articles, and twenty-seven book reviews. Although College Park obviously prepared me for a professorship in academia, I am very grateful to UMBC for providing me with a wonderful literary foundation that eventually led me to a long and successful career as a teacher and scholar.

After UMBC:

- Received M.A. and PhD in Comparative Literature at UMCP
- Worked as a technical writer and editor. Taught at University of Memphis in Department of English for 36.5 years

This Belongs to Larry Rosen '73, History

He Made Me Look!

Sometime between the Fall 1971 and Spring 1973 semesters, I saw a notice that Dr. John Money, the famous Hopkins sexologist, would give a talk on campus on the history of pornography. I hesitated in going, thinking I would be one of like five perverts in the whole huge lecture hall. When I got up the nerve to walk in, the place was packed! It was a good talk!

After UMBC:

- Taught history and other subjects in Baltimore City schools for 3 years
- After a teacher layoff and a year of unemployment and caddying for some cash, I got a job with the state of Maryland monitoring federal jobs programs.
- Due to a federal pilot program to automate the office's federal reporting system, we got a refrigerator-sized minicomputer with two disk drives the size of washing machines.
- Moved to the new computer unit of the office, became a systems analyst, writing data entry and reporting systems used by the office for the next 13 years.
- Moved to Florida when my wife got a job there in 1994
- Worked as a database administrator at a large Florida community college.
- Worked as an institutional research analyst until my retirement after 21 years in 2017.
- Learned about the campus natural environment, started a sustainability committee, advised some student clubs, and led occasional nature walks.
- Became active in Audubon and was president of the local chapter for 14 years.
- When asked what would be the optimal training for someone to become a research analyst, I responded, "Bachelor of Arts in History from UMBC."

Fun in Lecture Hall One

This Belongs to Gail Paige Williams Rouse '70, History

Perseverance

I do not remember when I first heard that there were plans to build another campus of University of Maryland to be located in Catonsville and opening in the fall of 1966. But when it was time to start applying to colleges I decided that I was going to attend UMBC. In fact, it may have been presumptuous of me because it was the only application that I submitted. I received my acceptance letter before the Christmas holiday of my senior year at Catonsville High School.

There were mainly three reasons why I made the decision to attend UMBC. The first reason was that the campus was located close to home. My family has lived for generations in the Black community located on and around Winters Lane. The campus was scheduled to be a commuter school and my family didn't have the funds for me to live away from home. Another reason was that I knew that a degree from a predominately white university would open doors for me when I stepped in the workforce. Most Historically Black Colleges and University (HBCUs) did not carry the prestige of its white counterparts in the 60's. And their graduates did not earn acknowledgements of the level and quality of their earned degrees as they entered into the workforce. However, the most important reason was that I strongly felt that there should be a Black presence in this predominately white institution.

I had been a product of forced desegregation of the Baltimore County Schools as a result of the Supreme Court ruling in 1954 of Brown vs. The Board of Education making separate but equal schools unlawful. I was bussed from my community starting at the 8th grade because it was determined by the county school board to dismantle Banneker Elementary/High School by eliminating a grade each year starting at the 12th grade. The Black students were absorbed into the white schools in Catonsville and surrounding areas. Banneker had been one of the only three schools in Baltimore County that offered a high school diploma for Black students for decades. Eventually Banneker School closed and was demolished.

Getting into the university proved to be the easier of the tasks; getting to the university campus was much more difficult. I was part of a one car, one driver family. My stepfather, the driver, worked at Fort Meade and had to be at work by 7a.m. Even though I lived only about seven miles away from the campus, there was no direct public transportation to get there. I would have had to walk a mile to the bus stop that would have taken me into the city, and then transferred to other buses to take me back in the county to a stop in Arbutus that was at least a mile away from the campus. This trip would have taken me at least two to three hours. I would have been taking this journey alone because no one else in my community was attending this university. And during the winter months, most of the journey would have been in darkness. It was a safety concern.

However, my community stepped up to solve this dilemma. My mother, aunts and other women of the community worked as domestics in the homes of white families in Catonsville. There were several male drivers in my community who provided transportation for these women to get back and forth to work daily according to their schedules and locations of the homes in which they worked. One of those drivers, whose name was Ben, decided to include me in his schedule and take me back and forth to school according to my schedule. Often the car would be full of these women who gladly added travel time to their schedules to accommodate my schedule. This took time away from their families, but they were willing to invest into my future. I am eternally grateful to them. This lasted for a year and I really felt sorry for the students who had to use public transportation and had to walk that long road to the campus in the wind, rain, mud, snow and bitter cold. Luckily for me, the following year my father bought me a car.

During the first weeks on campus, I remember that it rained and rained. We had to walk on boards that acted as sidewalks because there were none and the three that existed were in a building construction zone. There was the Student Union that housed the bookstore; the Multi-purpose building that included the gym and the cafeteria; and the Lecture Hall. The administration building was a pre-existing building on the campus that was located on Walker Ave. The registration process for classes took place there during the summer of 1966. We moved from desk to desk as faculty looked at our transcript and recommended classes. Our first identification cards were issued there.

The Black students soon found each other in a sea of 750 students moving around campus. There were only 19 of us and we very quickly created a bond amongst us. I was the only one that came from a predominately white high school and therefore did not feel as lost or isolated as many of the others felt. I was used to being the one and only Black in my classes. We soon created a social network and we visited each other's homes for many, many parties. We also attended social events on campus. One memorable event was when Otis Redding performed on campus. Another memorable event happened off campus at Turf Valley Country Club. It was a formal affair, and the 3 of us who entered the university in September, 1966 and graduated in 1970, attended the formal affair. It was Roslyn Harmon, myself, Gail Williams, and Beverly Rankin. Our escorts were James Rouse, who I met on campus in 1967 and later married in 1976 and have been married for 45 years, and Rodney, who was Beverly's escort; and Duke Allen, Roslyn's escort who she later married. The fourth Black female who graduated June, 1970 was Michelle Horsey who transferred in from College Park.

I worked for a brief time for the university as part of the recruiting program. We visited Baltimore City schools meeting with juniors who were contemplating applying to college. Individually we spoke about our reasons for attending UMBC and encouraged them to apply to a campus that was in its infancy and ensuring them that they could bring their points of view and influence to create a developing curriculum. In particular, I remember going to Forest Park and Edmondson High Schools because they were my introduction to predominately Black high schools.

There were only two Black professors that I remember in the first years. One was Dr. Low who was in the History department and taught Black History. The other professor was Dr. Brown who taught Music.

My major was American History with many credits also in American Politics. To aid in helping my parents pay my tuition, I applied for a state grant in which I committed to teach for two years. I was determined to be certified, but there was no Education major at UMBC. The philosophy was that to be a good teacher, you should have a major in a chosen subject matter. So the last two years I attended the Fall, Winter MiniMester, Spring and Summer school to acquire my state certification. The administration worked with me and others who were working toward state certification by providing projects on and off campus to meet our goals. I even took classes at Catonsville Community College.

Looking back, I am proud to be part of the legacy of UMBC.

After UMBC:

- Received a Master of Science in school administration from Johns Hopkins University.
- Taught elementary school grades 3 to 7 for 25 years in Baltimore City Public Schools.
- Managed a law office for 12 years.
- Married in 1976 to James Rouse who attended UMBC graduating from College Park.
- Mother of 2 sons, James and Luke.
- Grandmother of 4, James III, William, Violet and Blaire.

This Belongs to Carl Sallese '70, Biological Sciences

Something Happening Here

My perspective on the young UMBC may have been unique. I spent the first semester of my freshman year at College Park. There, the sprawling campus included about 35,000 students and I remarked that I didn't think I saw the same person twice! My classes could be a 15 or more-minute forced walk apart, because I was an Engineering major I was forced to enroll in ROTC and some classes were held on the 70's version of "remote learning". We sat in a classroom and watched on a TV monitor a professor who droned on remotely and we struggled to stay awake.

When I began my education at UMBC in February 1967, the institution couldn't have been more different. There were not more than a couple of hundred of us, everything, including the recently planted sod, was new and there weren't a lot of rules. Classes were small...even a class in the new Lecture Hall only included about 50-60 of us. We were all equal, middle class commuters from all over Baltimore. No big time sports heroes, no frats or sororities and, certainly, not much partying. But, because we were so few, we got to know each other even if that was only a smile and a nod. Our biggest sports were, as I recall, intramural flag football and softball in the spring. But the biggest difference was the interaction between teachers and us and, eventually, the administration. Many of them were not much older than we were and it was not unusual for us to speak with them before or after class and they were always available. Looking back, we enjoyed a progressive, small college experience at a state school and I think that was the incubator for the excellent institution UMBC has become today.

Thinking Outside the Lines

From the beginning, under the leadership of Chancellor Kuhn and Dean Schamp, UMBC chose to distinguish itself by becoming a leader among progressive State Universities. One attempt was an effort to examine the requirements for graduation and I was a student member of a Faculty Senate Subcommittee charged with reviewing current Maryland State policies and suggesting reforms at UMBC.

At that time, students were required to complete one or two courses in each major field of study: Science/Mathematics, Social Sciences, Modern and Classical Languages and Humanities/Fine Arts. In addition, specific requirements were set for degrees in any of those fields and the opportunity to reach across these areas was only through a number of credits in electives. In other words, degree requirements were extremely rigid and there was no consideration given for students to have input into structuring a degree program outside the lines.

The committee was composed of mostly young, forward thinking instructors who had recently graduated themselves and were sensitive to these, and other, inflexible, arbitrary graduation standards. For instance, at College Park, students were required to enlist in ROTC in order to earn an engineering degree. (I'm not sure if this applied to the few women at the time who were engineering students!) Committee members soon agreed that students should have a voice in their degree requirements and should be partners in planning a custom degree if they chose a non-traditional degree and began a plan to set new requirements. We presented our plan which created a new template for graduation requirements that allowed students more independence and introduced a new kind of degree, Interdisciplinary Studies, which was a revolutionary idea of the time. Credit for outside experience or independent studies was made possible.

Before becoming reality these new ideas needed approval of the Faculty Senate and I remember a heated meeting of the full Senate in the old lecture hall where the proposal was the changes presented by Committee Chairman Dr. Richard Roberts and Dr. William Mahaney. Of course, not everyone agreed with these progressive changes and it is certain that without the leadership of Dean Schamp, a forward-thinking faculty and the fact that UMBC was a new University that had not constructed silos around individual fields, the opportunity for personal choice in degree formation would not have succeeded. I'm not completely sure any of the changes made survive to this day but I did learn in a recent visit that there now are seven or so disciplines and students are required to select courses from each one. Things have changed!

After UMBC:

- Spent my adult life in retail purchasing and management
- Owned and operated several Ann Marie's Hallmark stores for 30 years. Retired in 2018
- Married in 1971 and recently celebrated 51 wonderful years together
- Adopted two daughters from Korea, one in 1983 and the second in 1985
- Currently enjoying 2 grandchildren along with trying to keep fit, cooking, some volunteer work, travelling and learning Italian
- "Greatest gifts from my UMBC education are self-reliance, working as part of a team to accomplish big things and the fact that the world really does want you to do something significant!"

This Belongs to Marty Schlesinger '71, Biological Sciences

Early Early Times

In the spring of 1966, I went to UMBC's Registrar's Office for information about the newly opening campus. My mother tagged along that morning and when we arrived at the Grey House early just before 8:00, the only person there was a gray-haired lady who introduced herself as Mrs. Wilson, Dr. Kuhn's secretary. She laughingly said the registrar, Mr. Turner, would probably be a little late and invited us to sit and talk. About then a rather big man came in with 2 cups of coffee and offered one to Mrs. Wilson and the other to my mother (who declined). Sipping his coffee, the gentleman introduced himself as "Guy Chisolm from Texas A and enema!"

For the next half hour, the two of them enthusiastically talked with me about my interests, the New UMBC campus, and the opportunities it would provide. By the time the registrar arrived, I was convinced that this was the place for me. After spending time with Mr. Turner, I was ready to apply. Before I left the building that morning, Mr. Chisolm also offered me a summer job.

Mrs. Wilson and Mr. Chisolm became very important people in not only my life, but my wife Jackie's. When classes began, Jackie, another student, worked for Mrs. Wilson in Dr. Kuhn's office and that is where I first met her. We remained close to both of them over the years and have very fond memories of our time spent with both Mr. Chisolm and Mrs. Wilson.

Mrs. Wilson and Mr. Chisolm were critical people in the startup and success of UMBC, remaining behind the scenes to ensure the campus ran smoothly and, along with Dr. Kuhn, engaging with students to make them know how important student views and thoughts were in forging a strong campus.

After UMBC:

- Received MS in Civil Engineering, University of Pittsburgh
- Career as Professional Process and Environmental Engineer spanning more than 50 years
- Principal and owner of Schlesinger Engineering, Inc., a civil and environmental engineering firm
- Married Jackie Davis who he met at UMBC
- Children, Dr. Kimberly Wyn Schlesinger, Martin Marc Schlesinger, Jr. CPA
- Grandchildren, 4
- Hobbies: Luthier, gardening, reading, hot air ballooning, Boy Scouts, and spending time with family and friends.
- Retired in Fredericksburg, Virginia

This Belongs to Robert Seasonwein '71, History

What's a UMBC?

I started college when I graduated in 1963 from high school in New York. In 1965 I enlisted in the Air Force, and because I had been a biology major with a chemistry minor, I was assigned to become a medic. Not just a medic, but a medical laboratory technician. The only problem with that was along the way I decided that becoming a doctor was not my calling, so I took a number of humanities courses in the service. When I was discharged in 1968, I returned to the East Coast and applied to College Park to complete my degree, now as a History major with an interest in political history. I arrived at the College Park registrar's office, ready to choose my class, but when the registrar learned that I was living in Columbia, he said that was a long commute, and "why don't you register at UMBC?" My response was, "What's a UMBC?"

Well, I did register at UMBC as a History major, and because I had already satisfied my degree requirements in the "hard sciences," I was able to focus on History, Political Science, Psychology, and Philosophy. Along the way, probably because I was somewhat older than many students, I also became friends with several professors. I finished my course work in December, 1970, completing 62 credits in three full semesters and one winter and summer semesters, enrolling at Syracuse University College of Law in 1971.

Two funny stories: While I was at UMBC, I rode a motorcycle. One day, as I was driving to school, I saw a man walking along the side of the road, and as I got closer, I saw that he was carrying a briefcase, and as I got even closer, I saw that it was Jim Arnold. I stopped and asked him if he wanted a ride, which he accepted. So Professor Arnold rode to UMBC on the back of my bike.

About five years ago, my older daughter, who has a PhD in Art History, moved from Princeton University, where she was on the faculty, to The University of Oregon's Museum of Art, where she became the Curator for Western Art (which included everything but Asian art.) One day she received a call from a professor who was planning to retire, and wanted her professional advice on his collection of Ulysses S. Grant lithographs. In the course of their discussion, she noted that one of the pieces was particularly nice, and asked where he had gotten it. He replied that he bought it in Maryland. Having grown up in Maryland, she asked what he was doing in Maryland, and he replied that he was teaching at UMBC. She said, "My dad went to UMBC," at which point he made the connection and asked if her father was Robert Seasonwein, and when she answered in the affirmative, he said that I was a student in the first class that he taught after getting his PhD. It was Jim Mohr. In addition to playing tennis in Columbia with him after I graduated, we reconnected when we came to visit our daughter and family in Oregon, and have had dinner with Jim and his wife on several occasions, and have a standing offer to go fly fishing whenever we visit.

So UMBC is no longer a small school, but it certainly is a small world, and whenever I am on campus, I am amazed what the "What's a UMBC" has become.

After UMBC:

- Graduated from Law School and worked for two government agencies (1974-77)
- Moved to Michigan and was a member of the legal staffs of two international corporations (1977-86)
- Moved back to MD to join DC office of NY Law Firm
- In 1991 joined the Criminal Division of the Department of Justice as a member of the Office of Special Investigation
- Worked and lived in Central Europe (2002-03)
- Received 1999 Distinguished Alumnus of the Year Award
- Left DOJ in 2004 for the legal staff at DHS/TSA.
- Retired from Government service in 2016 and started consulting practice.
- Prior to UMBC, Served in the U.S. Air Force 1965-68 and Married in 1968
- Two daughters, now 45 and 42, both married with children.

Plenty of Parking?

This Belongs to Lynne R. Sigler '70, Biological Sciences

A Compliment from Dr. Kuhn

I was chauffeured to UMBC, on September 19th, 1966, for the first day of class.

The ETA was about 8am. Ohhh… but not in a limousine. Oh no... a long bright yellow Baltimore County school bus with my mother as the chauffeur! (I had yet to get my driver's license) In the morning she dropped me off between her first and second run. I got to sit in the front seat. She stopped, opened the door and I got out… into a small grass swamp, which over the next few weeks would become big long mud trails covered over with plywood, which became mud covered plywood… in fact when it was time to select our mascot a group of us entered "PIGS" as a suggestion (not popular but true)... I thought it would never stop raining. No car or lockers, I had to lug books, binders and personal stuff around all day. Good exercise though, I lost about 30 pounds. I particularly looked forward to classes in Hillcrest, high on the hill, in the dungeon room… creepy place. What a hike! I think I had a Psych class with Diane Juknelis Tichnell there, phew. But, I digress. After a long day of going to classes and in between gathering in the cafeteria, I met up with the long yellow limo and my maternal chauffeur to go home and get ready to do it all over again… hmmm … sounds dismal and boring. Hardly!! Put a couple hundred freshmen, mostly graduates of high school around and within the beltway with an interesting new and experienced faculty, with some experimental and classical education concepts, in a fledgling university and anything can happen…UMBC was a cauldron of "growing pains"!!

When this project was announced, I started thinking about my UMBC experience and realized it had a significant effect on my ability to be able to shift into different situations when necessary. Class work was important but keeping your eyes and ears open is important to find or create opportunities and be willing to make adjustments. Here are some of the opportunities that were important to my time as a student and later in life…

– Attending the 2nd group to spend a weekend at the Donaldson Brown Center in the freshmen year. Dr. Joel Jones and Dr. Larry Lasher were two of the professors that weekend. Having access, in a relaxed environment, with these individuals reduces any fears you might have approaching them to discuss issues… they really are human. Dr. Jones gave me an "A" on a composition in English Writing because he was impressed with my unique but consistent punctuation.

– Entering the first "Talent Show" in December of 1966…(I took first place by the way). Dr. Albin O. Kuhn was in attendance. He said I remind him of Kate Smith.

– Worked on the technical crew of the first theatrical production of the drama department during the first year. "The Male Animal" by James Thurber and Elliott Nugent, 1940 Broadway play, also movie in 1942. This was my first theater experience and I learned a lot about non performing positions which helped when I was working in other theaters later in my life when I needed to work. Dana Levitz was one of the actors.

– I worked in the closet called the bookstore for a while as a freshman. I became very good at counting change. – Was approached in the senior year to work as a teaching assistant in the General Biology Labs.

– In Summer of 1970, after graduation, I filled in for Mr. Lou, the prep technician for all the Biology and Chemistry labs, when he took off for the Summer. Learned a lot of practical lab skills. – In the Fall of 1970 the present chairman of the Biology, Chemistry and Physics Departments, Dr. Martin Schwartz was proposing a graduate program for the division. Six individuals (5 students and one technician) matriculated through the Biochemical department of the graduate school, at the downtown campus but took courses that were being developed by the UMBC faculty, on the UMBC campus. Besides working as lab T.A.s we were all engaged in research projects. Lots of teaching but also learning design and execution of research experiments.

From UMBC I taught at a Baltimore County Community College for 15 years. Dr. Andrew Snope, who left UMBC to teach, like some of the other original faculty, because the philosophy of the importance of education over publishing or perish had changed, was teaching at the community college and he told me of a Biology faculty position available and encouraged me to come over and apply… I got the job. I've worked in a number of theaters over time in the Baltimore area as an actress, singer, costumer, in box offices and bar manager/tender since 1986. Other employment includes mosquito control for the Department of Agriculture, numerous temp jobs from entering case data in a bankruptcy department for a financial institution to driving cars in an auto auction, just to mention a few. I even taught in 1997 and 98 (thank you Bob Dietrich) as a lab instructor for General Biology and Anatomy and Physiology (It was great fun to work with some of my own professors…Carl Weber and John Kloetzel).

So, while I didn't end up as an astronaut nor a veterinarian, I think I've done OK. I am looking for another direction to go. That's my story and I'm sticking to it.

After UMBC:

- Became one of the first UMBC graduate students
- Taught at a Baltimore County Community College for 15 years
- Worked and acted in community theaters
- Worked as a lab instructor at UMBC in 1997-98

Many Different Ways to Commute

This Belongs to Jacques Smith '70, American Studies

Great Education and Experience

When I enrolled at UMBC I did so for pragmatic reasons. It was small and somewhat of a bargain because it was a commuter school. Somewhat like a community college but with a University ranking. I came from a blue collar family and it was hoped that I would be the first to receive a college degree. I was expected to work part time to make this happen. My first day at UMBC, was spent at the Hillcrest building where I, wearing a white shirt and tie, filled out paperwork, got my ID card, received my Class schedule, and met my advisor, Dr. Larry Lasher. He assured me that my scores were good, grades were good, and that I would be in his Advanced Literature class. He made me feel comfortable, but he forgot to tell me that he would require me to read a novel every week for all sixteen weeks of his class. This proved to be a major time management challenge!

I liked the campus! It was full of "newness" and energy. Construction was all around us and rumors of plans to make UMBC eventually larger than College Park told us that we were in on the beginning of something big. There were only three red brick buildings and lots of green spaces. We sometimes wondered if ivy would ever grow on the walls of those buildings, or if they would ever be named for a famous person, instead of Academic building I, or II, or Lecture Hall I. There was an old farm house where the administration worked, and there was an old silo in the field out in front of the cafeteria. It was easy to get to classes and downtime spent with friends in the cafeteria was fun and a good place to hang out, exchange ideas, play cards, or just relax.

I remember the rigor of the classroom instruction. I came from a small high school and did well there, but the classes that I took as a freshman at UMBC were very challenging. The professors were knowledgeable and fair. I learned very quickly that I had to up my game.

Socially, in that first year 1966-1967, I remember a few highlights. Our winter dance with Otis Redding, couldn't have been more fun. I enjoyed playing intramural basketball, especially when my team played the faculty team. Meeting new friends, eating lunch from a vending machine, and enjoying conversations with people from other places than where I grew up were all highlights for me.

After UMBC:

- Taught middle school language arts for 9 years
- Received a Master's Degree from Johns Hopkins University

- Served as a middle school Assistant principal and principal in Anne Arundel County for 34 years
- Curriculum Coordinator for incarcerated youths, staff developer, and advanced placement Grant administrator at MSDE- four years
- Member of UMBC adjunct faculty in the education department for 5 years
- Currently UMBC student intern supervisor
- Married to Cynthia for 44 years. One son - Matthew and one grandson – Ryan
- Retired and living on Maryland's Eastern Shore

Opening Day 1966   New School   New Friends

This Belongs to Rick (Rock) Soracoe '71, Economics

UMBC Baseball First Intercollegiate Victory

In September 1966, UMBC opened to wide eyed co-ed freshman not knowing what to expect from our new high school plus one. We found a lot of mud, plywood thrown over the mud, and three (3) buildings (gym/cafeteria, lecture hall, and administration with classrooms and the library). We found a faculty that was young and eager to impart their knowledge, and the faculty and students were going to experience growing pains together.

My story will be about a 1st for the university in the sports field. The 1st sports team put together in the fall of 1966 was the men's soccer team. Remember Title IX had not come in yet, and there were no women's sports teams, until my classmate Linda Lyall Sowers got with athletic director, Dick Watts, and formed women's field hockey, basketball, and lacrosse teams for the 1967-68 school year. The 1st men's soccer team was not good going 0-5 in that fall of 1966, but coach Tom Rider saw some potential as two (2) years later they posted an 8-1-2 record, which stood for many years as the highest winning percentage of any UMBC sports team. The 1st men's basketball team was also not very good, going 0-21. (I'm sure some of my basketball guys will comment on this.) Coach John Frank was preparing for the future.

Tom Rider prepared a pretty raw baseball squad and the lacrosse team was predicted to be pretty good, so it was a race to see which team would win The BIG ONE. I'm proud to say baseball won on April 8 1967 beating Catonsville Community College 3-2 in a nine (9) inning complete game by both pitchers. I was the winning pitcher and Ken Diehl, who later pitched for UMBC and was my roommate on Dr. Sherwin, Dr. Storch, and Dr. Freyman's 1st MiniMester trip to Europe, was the hard luck loser as his team committed four (4) errors behind him. It was a beautiful sunny spring day and we played the game at Banneker field in Catonsville because UMBC didn't have a home field. I don't remember much about the game except that I still have the box score from The Sun Papers and that I have bragging rights over my brother-in-law who played 3rd base for CCC in that game (he did get one (1) hit). Lacrosse won their 1st game shortly thereafter, but baseball claimed win #1. I would like my baseball teammates from 1967 to fill me in on more details about UMBC's 1st intercollegiate victory as I have the box score but not much else.

After UMBC:

- Worked 51 years in the lighting industry and am retiring on 4/15/22

- Married Charlotte Buschman class of 1972. Char taught in Carroll County for ten (10) years, Baltimore County for twenty one (21) years, CCBC for three (3) years, and still tutors children in math.
- She taught Dr. Walter Sherwin's grandchildren in school
- We have two (2) children with two (2) grandchildren and one (1) grandchild on the way
- Still residing in Catonsville
- I have four (4) holes-in-one in golf and pitched a no hitter in baseball

UMBC Baseball and Soccer

This Belongs to Louie Lyall Sowers '70, American Studies

Retriever Hall of Fame

I came to UMBC in 1966 as a freshman. I have nothing but great memories of those early days. Most of those memories have to do with playing sports. I played volleyball as a sophomore (no women's sports in freshman year,) and then field hockey, basketball, and volleyball in my junior and senior years. I also was the scorekeeper for the men's basketball team. My sophomore year we had no uniforms, so we wore our gym uniforms. Halfway through the field hockey season in the following year, we got uniforms. We wore those same uniforms for all three sports. We also had the same coach, Joan Chenoweth for all three sports. She was a great coach who developed a close rapport with all the girls. I developed great friendships with my fellow team members, and have stayed friends with many of those women even to this day, fifty years later. I can remember having an "all-night sports night" in the gym one year. Coach Chenoweth was the chaperone and we just stayed up all night and played fun games like crab soccer. We established a Women's Athletic Association, designed charm bracelets as athletic awards, and had an awards banquet. We became a close knit group, and although we didn't always have a winning record, our basketball team in my senior year was invited to the State Championships and we were seeded second. Quite an accomplishment for such a young school.

In addition to sports, I can remember hanging out in the cafeteria between classes and playing cards, having Friday afternoon mixers in the cafeteria, walking on plywood between buildings before the sidewalks were in place, raft contests in the library lake, and enjoying great relationships with the faculty. Most of them were not that much older than we were and it seemed to present a unique opportunity that I can't imagine happens in most universities.

Being one of the pioneers of UMBC is something I will always cherish and remember with great pride and affection.

After UMBC:

- Enjoyed a career as librarian in academic, commercial, and public libraries.
- Retired in 2012.
- Inducted into the UMBC Athletic Hall of Fame.
- Married Greg Sowers, September, 1987
- Lives in Bowley's Quarters.

This Belongs to Rene Stiebing '73, English

Two UMBC's and a Legacy

I started at UMBC in February 1967, the second semester it was open, having transferred from Salisbury State College, a VERY traditional state college. Salisbury had housemothers in the dorms, dress codes – no pants on campus until after 7 PM, and freshmen wore beanies. Transfer to UMBC – who is going to tell Veterans to wear beanies… Dress codes? I remember Dr. Shedd coming to class barefoot! I was in culture shock.

At Salisbury everyone held on to "where you were from". Western shore kids, Eastern shore kids Catholics, Baptists … At UMBC everyone was "there", and very much in the present. In Salisbury, the college held a candle vigil for the Vietnam conflict with a professor lecturing about the history of the conflict and the US involvement. UMBC had protests, bomb threats, news reporters on campus.

Don't think Salisbury was dull. There was the time some "boys" snuck a 5 foot long iguana into the "girl's" dorm hallway in the middle of the night.

Two different UMBCs

I experienced two different UMBCs. The first was in February 1967 when I transferred in. The school was NEW. The "cafeteria" was on the ground floor below the gym. It offered vending machines with junk food. There were also lots of metal tables and chairs that were usually filled with students either chatting or playing cards. Since the campus was so new and everyone commuted, it was the only game in town. The other options were in class or in the library which was located on the third floor of the classroom building. I don't remember what that building was called, but it also housed a very small bookstore in the basement.

In addition to Academic Building 1, classes were also held in the "administration" building at the top of the hill on Walker Avenue. It was a hike up to class, especially if you had back to back classes up the hill and then down in the Academic building and then up the hill. The path between the two buildings was a wind tunnel that seemed to be 100 degrees, ok, 50 degrees, above or below the actual temperature, depending on the season.

There were some great concerts held in the gym. I remember performances by Otis Redding and Charlie Byrd. Very different but both wonderful events.

The second UMBC for me was after I married, had a child and returned to UMBC as a part-time student. Money was tight so I made sure I received every minute of education I was paying for. That meant I became "the adult who sits in the front row, has done all the assignments, answers questions thoughtfully and usually correctly, asks challenging questions, and NEVER MISSES CLASS." I'm sure most people hated me.

Child care was a struggle so I often brought my 18 month old with me and handed her off to my best friend for the hour I was in class. Donna entertained Sandy by riding the elevator with her, up and down and up and down, because Sandy loved to push the buttons. I think Sandy loved it and it also was a great way for Donna to meet guys. My younger sister, Diane and her at the time boyfriend Rick, were also students there. Diane would also entertain Sandy, but I don't think they rode the elevators. However, one day Rick "borrowed" Sandy and took her to his professor's office to ask for an extension on a paper because "his wife was sick and he had to take care of Sandy." He got the extension.

As time passed I increased the number of classes I took until I was full time. To offset the cost of child care, I volunteered at Sunshine School, the child care center started by Dr. Trudy Hamby and a group of UMBC folks. The center continues today as the Catonsville Presbyterian Family Child Care Center. Back at UMBC I was taking classes for certification in Early Childhood Education – no surprise there. On occasion, I would take Sandy to the Early Childhood Lab classes and, as we students practiced the activities we would teach in our field placements, Sandy would also participate in the activities. It was great learning and fun for all of us. I believe that when I graduated, Sandy had clocked more hours in Early Childhood classes than some graduating students.

Sandy finally did graduate from UMBC in May 1986 with a degree in Film and Video.

After UMBC:

- Taught kindergarten at Mount Providence Child Development Center.
- With my husband Bob, spent the next 8 years as house parents at Milton Hershey School in Hershey, PA. During that time we cared for and parented 66 children ages 4 through 14. It was an extraordinarily wonderful experience!
- Returned to the Baltimore area where I was Program Director for a Head Start Research, Training and Demonstration project focusing on brain-based theories of learning and earned my M.Ed. through UMUC.
- Beginning in 1986 I worked for Baltimore City and then the Maryland State Department of Human Resources as Assistant Chief for Day Care Licensing for Baltimore City, Supervisor of Family Child Care registration, and as Program Supervisor for Maryland's subsidized child care voucher program.
- Worked at the Maryland State Department of Education monitoring implementation of improvement plans developed by Baltimore City Public Schools identified as reconstitution eligible.

- Retired in 2013 as a Regional Administrator for Special Education working with local school systems.
- Married for 54 years to Bob Stiebing, 2 daughters, 2 grandchildren
- "My entire career has been focused on providing support and services to children and their families. UMBC prepared me well."

UMBC Student Teacher in the Classroom

This Belongs to Diane Juknelis Tichnell '70, Political Science

When the Smoke Clears…

When the campus first opened in 1966, it was necessary to use the windowless rooms as classrooms in the basement of the administration building known as Hillcrest. In spite of the inability to open windows, smoking was permitted and there were ashtrays provided for student use at each seat and one for the instructor at the desk.

Our instructor would light up a cigarette at the beginning of her lecture and would chain smoke for the entire class session, squashing those tiny cigarette stubs into the ashtray and immediately lighting up another one. A number of students also followed suit. By the end of class time, the room was filled with an amount of smoke that often made it difficult to see any notations made on the blackboard.

Because all of us were exposed to similar situations in other classrooms and lecture halls, no one noticed the odor left on our clothes as everyone else's had the same smoke smell. My parents, however, would ask me regularly when I returned home if I had taken up the smoking habit myself. Second-hand smoke was not much of a concern in the Good Old Days.

Better Late than Never

In January of 1969, UMBC's MiniMester was in full swing. Several of my UMBC classmates had gone to Europe on a tour with several faculty from the Ancient Studies Department to Italy, France and Great Britain. This was no walk in the park as they had plenty of work to do to earn their credits for the semester. I was not able to join them in this exciting venture as the Retriever newspaper was assembling a special issue featuring all candidates for the upcoming Student Government Association elections. I was editor of the newspaper at that time and the publication process was primitive compared to today.

I managed to break away for a brief trip to Massachusetts to visit relatives and timed the trip and my flight home to coincide with the UMBC students' return flight from Europe. I thought it would be a real kick to hear all about their adventures and perhaps write a story or two for the Retriever as we flew back together.

After a full day of touring Boston with a family member, I made my way to the airport, checked my bags except for one small train case, and positioned myself in a comfortable waiting area near a flight arrival board. The flight with my UMBC friends was on time and all looked great for my big surprise! At the appropriate time I made my way to the arrival gate and watched the plane roll to a stop.

Snow had begun to fall a short time before the plane had landed. As the bleary eyed travelers made their way up the gangway, I stood waving with a big smile and suddenly was mobbed by my traveling buds! What a moment!

As I explained to my friends how I had come to be in Boston, the snow storm greatly intensified, becoming a blizzard. One by one, outgoing flights were being canceled. Feverishly, passengers watched the departure board and to their dismay, eventually saw all flights, with the exception of our TWA flight to Baltimore, canceled! With great relief, my traveling friends were able to board safely and waited for me to join them. To save money, I had opted for a student standby ticket which meant that after all regular passengers were boarded, the remaining seats were awarded to students in the order in which they had checked in. One wrinkle to this process was a show stopper for me. Regularly ticketed passengers from other airlines' canceled flights were given seats on the TWA flight, reducing the number of seats available for student standby. I missed the flight by one seat. I waved good-bye to my UMBC friends and to my luggage as they both took off in the blizzard.

My train case and I made our way back to my family via Greyhound bus in a small town 60 miles from Boston for an additional stay. My UMBC traveling friends were diverted to the airport in Philadelphia and eventually bussed back to Baltimore's Friendship Airport in the wee hours of the morning. One of the travelers had to have her hard contact lenses surgically removed from her eyes as a result of the extended length of time she was forced to wear them.

Assignment: Facing a Challenge

As a cub reporter for the Retriever newspaper in 1968, my editor Mike Klingaman sent me on an assignment to attempt a personal interview with the leader of a group coming on campus in the afternoon to enlist members and support. Bobby Seale, co-founder of the Black Panther Party for Self-Defense, would be speaking in the Student Union Building. Maybe he would be available to talk with me privately before the rally began.

As I approached the inner doors of the meeting room about 45 minutes prior to the rally start, two very imposing men in fatigue style dress, bearing weapons, stood at the entrance. I asked in a rather shaky voice if it was possible to speak with Bobby Seale for a few minutes. Without responding, one of the men threw open the door and walked to the front of the meeting room where I could briefly see Bobby conversing with some people in the front row before the door closed.

My next recollection is of both men at the door escorting me to the front of the meeting room to a waving, bright smiling Bobby Seale who asked me "What can I do for you, Little Sister?" For the next half hour, Bobby Seale and I were the only two people in the room as far as he was concerned. I had a page full of questions to ask him and he answered every one in detail, only looking away from me when pondering a response. I wrote furiously, not wanting to miss a word as he gave me the history to date of the Black Panther Party which he and Huey Newton had co-founded in 1966. He talked of the Party members educating themselves on laws at the federal, state and local levels, of monitoring law enforcement activities and reports of police brutality, and of his vision for pursuing justice for those incarcerated without due process. His friend and co-founder, Huey Newton, had been arrested and was awaiting a hearing on charges related to a demonstration.

I found myself seeing with new eyes what real commitment to an ideal meant. Bobby Seale was a man in his thirties with a wife and family in California, traveling boldly with a mission and a vision, putting himself in danger coming from many different directions. He appeared calm and steady with his gaze, but enthusiastic and fully committed with his words. He changed my entire focus from the small protected community of UMBC to the rising tide of no longer settling for the status quo by many in our country. My cub reporter news writing began to mature as Bobby Seale and I concluded the one on one interview. The room was full with students standing against the walls. His message was clear and no one would leave the rally unchanged by his call to boldly stand up for what was right. His journey would take twists and turns and the Black Panther Party for Self-Defense would ultimately not survive the turmoil from within itself.

Bobby Seale has never stopped pursuing his vision for justice. In 2016, at the 50th anniversary of the UMBC campus opening, I emailed Bobby Seale to thank him for opening my eyes to a less parochial vision of life in this country. He continues to lecture and to support causes for justice in his eighties. If you want to see a portion of the hard road he chose to travel, do not miss the movie The Trial of the Chicago 7.

After UMBC:

- Worked in UMBC University Relations 1970-71
- Received MS in Information Systems Johns Hopkins University 1997
- Career in Finance and Information Technology 1979-2016
- Married in 1971 and gifted with daughter born in 1972
- Lives in Catonsville with resident grandson graduating from UMBC in May 2022
- Active in Toastmasters International

This Belongs to Stan Turk '73, Psychology

The Unknown Student

One of my favorite stories is having my photo published in the Retriever.

However, I never saw the photographer, and they never asked my name. So the caption simply identified me as an "unknown student!"

After UMBC:

- Traveled around the country playing music for about two years
- Returned to Baltimore playing music full-time until 1987
- Graduated from law school at night and practiced law until 2017
- Served 20 years with the Maryland Attorney General's office
- After retiring in 2017, I found music again and have been performing locally with several talented groups.

Page 12 The Retriever April 18, 1972

Photo by Skip Boyd

SPRINGTIME STRIKES UMBC
An unknown student sets sights high as he braves the trees, buildings, and poles in search of a release from the tensions of being a college student.

Unknown Student Identified

This Belongs to Bill Wade '72, Economics

Basketball and Beyond

One of these memories was being selected to the UMBC basketball team in 1969 and having the opportunity to play Division 1 College Basketball. I did not go out for the Poly High School Team. I did try out for the Community College of Baltimore Team but was cut at the last cut. Thus, when I arrived at UMBC in 1969, my confidence was not at a high level. After several weeks of tryouts, the final cuts were made and I found my name on the list of players that had made the team. Obviously, I was quite excited to have accomplished my goal of making the team.

We did not win many games during my 3 years playing for UMBC but the many friendships gained, the added skills learned, and the competition of playing against top players from Universities in Maryland, Virginia and Pennsylvania was the highlight of my athletic career. We had many exciting road trips but a few specific trips have special meaning.

We traveled to Westminster, MD to play Western Maryland College, now McDaniel College. As a young boy, my father used to take me to the college to watch the Colts practice. We would watch the morning practice grab some lunch including some homemade ice cream and head back to take in the afternoon practice. It always seemed like a long ride to Westminster. Then, in 1977 my wife Bridget and I built a house in Westminster and for the next 10 years I drove to work in Baltimore. So I guess it was not such a long ride after all. By the way I met my wife Bridget while at UMBC on a blind date arranged by Carol and Jack Mullen. We will celebrate our 48th anniversary.

Another exciting trip took us to Johnstown, Pa. Johnstown is known as the Flood city due to the many disastrous floods that the City has encountered over the years. This trip in 1971 was going to be our first overnight trip. Johnstown was about 3 hours away from Catonsville. We were looking for a win on the court, a nice dinner and perhaps a little party in our rooms. There was also a chance of a big snowstorm. 1971 was also the first year UMBC fielded a Freshman team. Emmerson Small and John Chatham were recruited to the team in 1970. They were good players and were the leaders of the Frosh team. Coach Frank promoted them to the Varsity team about mid-way through the season. They played for the Varsity team in Johnstown.

Unfortunately, our plan did not go well. We got blown out in both games. Coach Frank was so upset over the Refs calls that he received several technical fouls and was tossed from the Varsity game. Coach Frank was so pissed that he ordered us onto the bus and we headed directly for Catonsville in a driving rainstorm. We stopped along the way for a restroom break, some gas and some snacks. Many of the players thought it would be a healthy dinner to eat ice cream. So we purchased some half gallons, got some spoons and shared our treats on the way home. Can you imagine trying these eating habits with the current CDC guidelines?

I didn't know at the time that Bridget was born and raised in Johnstown. We were married in Johnstown in July of 1973 on one of the hottest days of record. Many of the players on the team joined us at the wedding. We finally did have our party. During subsequent years we made many trips to Johnstown. Of particular interest to me was the Holiday Basketball Tournament hosted by Johnstown every Christmas. I enjoyed attending these games and watching great teams from Detroit, New York, Philadelphia, Baltimore and DC. Many future NBA stars played in the games including Wilt Chamberlain and Adrian Dantley.

The most important memory from my years at UMBC were the friendships developed and maintained since our graduation. Richard and Karen Hammock have remained friends for 50 years. We also stayed in touch with many of the original Fab Four group (now known as the Founding Four). Many thanks go out to Gary Rupert and Jack Mullen for coining the phrase and working to maintain communications between the group and scheduling periodic activities where we could still get together. We still have a small group of Fab Four members including Richard, Jack, Linda Dunn, Louie and I who with the help of Cheryll Ratzsch from UMBC have managed to stay in touch in recent years. Hopefully, we can enjoy continued communications and contacts in the years ahead and also continue to stay up on UMBC's academic and Athletic accomplishments.

After UMBC:

- Landed a job at Monumental Life Insurance Company in Baltimore, started one month after graduation and began a 40 year career in the Life and Health Insurance Industry.
- Active in Insurance Education Programs and earned numerous Insurance Education Designations during my career. Became active in local and National Insurance Organizations, served on numerous Committees, and was elected President of National Organizations including the International Claim Association.
- After playing on the UMBC Basketball team, I continued to play basketball for 30 years with some of the players who were on the team.
- Met my wife Bridget while at UMBC on a blind date arranged by Jack and Carol Mullen. Married for almost 50 years.
- After losing contact with UMBC following graduation, I subsequently was able to get reacquainted with UMBC graduates through the Fab Four group. I have remained friends with members of this group and stay current with UMBC accomplishments and activities.

This Belongs to Greg Walker '73, Biological Sciences

Lucky Ducks

Once upon a time there was a contest to name the ducks that lived in the library pond.

At the time, all buildings were numbered – Academic 1, 2, and 3; Gym 1, 2; and Dorms 1, 2, and 3.

I was inspired to submit my names for the ducks:

Duck 1

Duck 2

Duck 3

I won the contest.

After UMBC:

- Graduated from U of Maryland School of Medicine 1978 and finished MD specialty training in 1981.
- Started and continue to have a solo private practice in Roland Park in Internal Medicine.
- Part-time faculty at Hopkins School of Medicine for 33 yrs.
- Married 37 years to OB GYN Nurse Professor at Catonsville Community College.
- Two children grown standing on their own two feet. Greg Jr. gets married in October.
- UMBC was the greatest choice. I left in 1973 with great memories, a lifetime of great friends, and a superb education.

UMBC Wildlife

This Belongs to Rona Rosen Warner '70, American Studies

To Europe and Home with 50 Cents

I remember my first year of college, living with my sister and commuting to University of Maryland, College Park. I remember the first day of school, meeting in a very large auditorium and having a speaker tell us to look right and look left knowing that by the end of four years two of us would no longer be enrolled in the University. The experience was pretty unsettling. To add to that, most of my friends were living in dorms and I felt like an outsider. Most of my classes there were huge...taught in a large, impersonal auditorium where notes were displayed on a large screen. I remember feeling very lost...

After a year there, my sister got a job in California and I was back living with my parents in their home in Baltimore. I can't say I was upset about leaving College Park but I also wasn't excited about entering UMBC, which I knew very little about except that it was brand new, I would be in the first graduating class, and my credits from College Park would all be transferred.

I entered UMBC in the fall of 1967. It was a bit strange entering as a sophomore. I didn't know anyone. I didn't have a car. And there were no buses that rode from my house to campus. I don't exactly know how I got to and from school every day...

I wanted to be a teacher but education was not considered a major. So I became an American Studies major and also took courses in education in order to earn a teaching certificate. Being a student in Joel Jones' and Ed Orser's American Studies classes was the highlight of my years at UMBC. Both of them really opened me up to so many new ideas! I found them to be teachers who were passionate and knowledgeable about their subject area and extremely personable and available to their students. Quite a contrast from my experience at College Park!

I don't remember how I met Bonnie Hurwitz. I suppose it was through being an American Studies major with her. In our junior years, we decided to become housemates. We rented an apt in a house not far from campus. We became great friends. This was more like the college experience I was hoping for... more independence. I don't remember how we paid for food. When I went home, my mother would send bags of food for us, including her homemade vegetable soup. When Bonnie returned from a visit with her aunt she always came back with salmon cakes and macaroni and cheese which we ate every night for a week.

Another peak experience was traveling during a winter "MiniMester" to England, France, and Italy taking a course offered from the history department titled "Ancient and Modern Rome". Never having been out of the country before, this was quite an eye opener for me. I remember coming back with 50 cents in my pocket!!

I spent a lot of time in the cafeteria between classes. There wasn't much else to do and I didn't have a car to go home. So I would do a lot of snacking and studying there. After classes, I would go to my job at the reception desk for the offices of the teachers in the education department. One of the teachers, Janet Carsetti, became instrumental in helping me find a teaching job at an elementary school in Anne Arundel County. I ended up teaching in that county for 41 years!

I remember Abbie Hoffman coming to campus after being invited by an American Studies student named Jack Walsh. I remember how exciting it felt to see someone with international fame speak about the Vietnam War at our little local college. I remember being on the staff of the Red Brick newspaper and being afraid that my parents would see how radical it was both politically and culturally. During the graduation ceremony, the Red Brick staff distributed copies of the newspaper to guests of the graduates. I remember wondering not only what my parents would say but also if I might not be allowed to graduate off the stage because of the contents of that newspaper!

Abbie Hoffman at UMBC

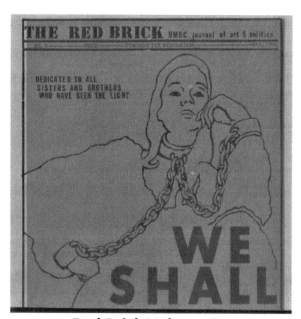

Red Brick Volume 2

This Belongs to Maryrose Whelley '72, English

DIY Spirit

I went to UMBC because it was close to home, simple to apply to, and my parents could afford the books and tuition. I'd seen my high school friends agonize over getting accepted at the school of their choice and then agonize over affording room, board, and tuition at the places where they got accepted. I did not want to go through that. UMBC was part of the U of Maryland system and that was good enough for me. Plus my brother was just a year younger and my sister was 4 years younger so there was the potential for years with the expense of more than one kid in college at the same time.

I heard Ed Berlin speak at UMBC's 50th celebration. He described the DIY spirit at the school in those early years and looking back I agree with him. The faculty and staff were not much older than the students in many cases and we were all willing to take a chance on this new liberal arts campus.

1968-1969

For Orientation and Registration in the summer of 1968, the incoming 1st year students were bussed to DBC (Donaldson Brown Center) in Port Deposit MD. It was a lovely setting. For some reason, I did not wear my name tag at first which lead to some confusion about what my role was. For a short time I was assumed to be one of the orientation staff. And this was OK with me.

I went back to DBC at least one other time for a retreat. In those early years DBC had the very civilized option of letting you 'work off' your fairly modest room and board by doing light cleaning and other chores.

In my 1st year, one of the students had a job at a donut factory in Ellicott City. They brought in big brown paper grocery bags of the discard donuts and left them in the commuter cafeteria for anyone who wanted them. My impression looking back was we were not a wealthy student body and many students had part time jobs, maybe even fulltime jobs, to help with their expenses.

My last Spanish instructor for my GDR (General Distribution Requirement) was an older woman, Olga Ferrer, from Spain who was in Spain during Franco's dictatorship and was anti-Franco. At the time I thought this was wildly exotic.

In the Fall semester I had my 1st English class with Dr. William Mahaney. I had tested out of the required 1st year comp class and ended up in his 2nd level lit class. He asked me why I was in that class and after I explained he said "OK" but

I needed to learn what a 'comma splice' was and how not to use it. I never really learned that but I came to like him as a person and a teacher.

I think this was the academic year Tim Buckley played a concert in the gym. (The only large performance space UMBC had at the time.) Earth Opera opened for him. We just sat on the floor, no chairs. Now he is better known as Jeff Buckley's father. Then he was a singer songwriter with a multi-octave voice range. I am so glad I got to see him.

Sometime this year I got a job at Silber's Bakery working on the weekends, mostly Sundays. Another student told me they were hiring. I kept this job for a few years.

More importantly, sometime in my first year at UMBC, I got a job on campus in the Admissions and Registrations office. I do not remember how I heard about the job BUT it eventually lead to my first and second post-graduation full time jobs. AND those jobs eventually lead to my decision to change careers away from 'the helping professions' and into what was then called DP (data processing). The wonderful Jim Milani was one of my co-workers. He and his equally wonderful spouse Liz helped me get hired by a local company that ran their own DP training class. All of this led to a much better fit for me career wise.

1969-1970
Winter Session: I went on the Ancient Studies trip to London, Italy, and Paris. The chaperones were Dr. Eve Parrish and Dr. Walt Sherwin. I was at the airport when I got my grades for the Fall semester and found out I made Dean's List. I was so excited I called my parents from a phone booth to tell them.
When we were in Florence I went to bed early while others went out dancing. My friends thought I should not miss out on all of the fun so they called our hotel with a fiction about 'eminent arrest, please come now and bail us out' that sent me into the night to rescue them only to find it was all a humbug. The trip was my first time on a plane, first time out of the US. It gave me a taste for travel that I have to this day.

The first dorm opened with no food service. We got by on cheese sandwiches sold by a fellow student and whatever we could cook in the common room for our floor. My suitemate was the child of Holocaust survivors and an ardent supporter of Israel. We had a poster of Moshe Dayan on our bathroom wall. It was an interesting way to be greeted when we stepped out of the shower.

UMBC had demonstrations in May 1970 against the Cambodia bombing and the shootings at Kent State and Jackson State. The College Park campus also had much larger demonstrations. One afternoon a contingent of the Maryland

National Guard headed for UMCP stumbled into UMBC instead. They figured out fairly quickly they were in the wrong place, turned around, and left.

I spent the summer session in the dorms working with registration. I was planning to transfer elsewhere in the Fall. And Dr. William Mahaney was also moving on. In order to take one last class with this favorite teacher, he approved me for a 4th year level class on King Lear. It was fun.

1970-1971
Elsewhere

1971-1972
I came back in the Fall of 1971 and resumed my student job in the Admissions and Registrations office in the Summer of 1971. I was amazed by how much bigger the campus seemed than when I left just a year ago, both in number of students and number of buildings. This year I lived at home and concentrated on graduating on time.

After UMBC:
- Started out working in Student Services at UMBC.
- By 1976 I knew the 'helping professions' were not for me so with the help of UMBC Student Services I identified Information Technology as a good career fit.
- My job at UMBC allowed me to take a few relevant courses while still working (there was no UMBC IT degree at that time). A UMBC contact led to my first IT job.
- Along the way I made good use of my writing and reasoning skills acquired courtesy of my UMBC English degree.

First New Dorm Residents Move In

This Belongs to Larry Wilder '70, Biological Sciences

Sole Man

In order to earn money to go to UMBC my experience at Westview Mall covered a lot of ground. My most important work was at Westview Liquors (1963-74), which was owned and managed by my father Sidney and his brother Erv. My mother Barbara worked there routinely throughout the years - as did I - especially around the holidays during the gift rush. My sister Gail was an occasional visitor, and she did work at Hutzler's after her high school graduation.

Aside from work at the liquor store, there were other jobs occupying my time away from school. In junior year, I put time in at both Baker's and Kavanaugh's. There was also a job at G.E.M. further out on Route 40. All of these positions assisted with my expenses for the school's first MiniMester trip to Europe in early 1969.

My final extracurricular job there was at Hahn's during senior year, the year of the second MiniMester trip that I also attended. The assistant manager was Harry Shames. He was an older man with glasses and a full head of dark hair parted neatly on one side. Since he was not always there when I was, my interaction with him was limited.

There was one other thing about him that I remember vividly even now. During the attempt to sell pairs of shoes to a customer, either the manager or the assistant manager was needed to confirm the proper fit. "Long enough and wide enough" was the verbal verification that someone like me on commission always liked to hear. I can easily picture hearing him say that - even the instances that took place when he was on the opposite side of the store.

Prelude to the First MiniMester Trip

The second half of my time at UMBC included taking an art history course in the fall semester of my junior year. The text used was *History of Art* by H. W. Janson.

When the opportunity to travel to Europe in the school's first MiniMester term in early 1969 was announced, several factors came to mind. Two of them follow.

My experience away from home was quite limited. During the summer of 1964 I went on a trip with the Lancers Boys Club to the New York World's Fair, baseball's Hall of Fame in Cooperstown, Niagara Falls, and a cluster of small towns across the Canadian border in Ontario. It was the summer of A Hard Day's Night, the Beatles' first film and movie album.

Curiosity played a part. With many European landmarks displayed in the Art History book, seeing some of them would enhance the course's content.

A personal objective was met by seeing pictures in the text book evolve into three-dimensional structures. The following abbreviated list has one landmark per city visited: St. Paul's Cathedral (London), St. Peter's Basilica (Vatican City), the Colosseum (Rome), the Church of St. Francis (Assisi), the Church of St. Maria del Fiore (Florence), and Notre Dame Cathedral (Paris).

Going on the first trip in January, 1969 provided a benefit that nobody would have expected. On Sunday, January 12, the sports world was rocked when the New York Jets shocked the heavily favored Baltimore Colts in Miami with a 16-7 victory in Super Bowl III. Watching "Yours, Mine, and Ours" on a rainy night in the Eternal City was infinitely better than what our friends and relatives had to endure. The saying "Better Rome than home" made its way through the group.

There were two brushes with fame, the first a lot more expected than the second. During the first trip, a visit was scheduled in advance for a papal audience. By putting myself next to the aisle in St. Peter's Basilica, I had an up close and personal view of Pope Paul VI being carried on a throne that was verified by the slides that were later developed. In January, 1970, a sighting even more up close and personal occurred by chance in downtown Athens. Outside of a store stepped Jackie Onassis, just over six years after her life-changing day in Dallas. With camera in hand, I snapped a few pictures from where I was close enough to see her smile. (Little did I know that later that year - my first as a dental student at the University of Maryland, School of Dentistry - I would have been able to label each tooth that showed up in the slides.)

The experiences of MiniMester trips in successive years gave me the knowledge and confidence to return to Italy about forty times from 1986 through 2010. While I still maintain contacts by regular mail, emails, and phone calls with friends in different cities met in that period I still read my diary on a daily basis each January for both trips. Older and newer memories are still valued.

After UMBC:
- Received DDS from University of Maryland School of Dentistry 1975
- Solo dental practice in Eldersburg (1977-2013)
- Solo dental practice in Randallstown (2013-2020)
- Radio show on KFNX-AM (Phoenix AZ 2000-2001) - highlight of one-hour live interview with Joe Garagiola, former "Today Show" host and member of the 1946 World Champion St. Louis Cardinals
- Radio show on WQLL-AM (Baltimore 2006-2015)
- Forty trips to Italy (1986-2010)

This Belongs to Linda Williams '71, American Studies

Playin' and Singin'

My true UMBC experience didn't really begin until my sophomore year. Since I didn't have a car, I had to spend so much time commuting from northeast Baltimore by bus or bumming rides, and working at Hutzlers downtown, that I didn't get involved in on campus activities during my freshman year.

As a sophomore, however, I met a new friend who encouraged me to join the newly formed women's sports teams. They desperately needed players, so although I had never played field hockey or basketball, and only had intramural volleyball experience, I jumped into the fray. There was a mix of some very talented players and newbies like me. I spent most of my three years on the bench for basketball, but I was pretty good at volleyball, and I got a Most Improved Player award for field hockey that first year. (It was kind, but I think doing anything right would have been an improvement.) However, with the determination of our coaches and the women athletes, the teams improved considerably by the time I graduated.

In my junior year I also had the good fortune to become a member of another new organization on campus. I joined the UMBC Chorus in 1969, under the direction of Dr. Marian Brown, with that same friend who got me into sports. (Turnabout is fair play, right?). We were not seasoned vocalists, but we loved to sing and learn, and with Dr. Brown's patience, talent, and inspiration, we did become a chorus. We performed several concerts on campus for the two years I was there, and we tried our best to sing "Aquarius" for the 1970 graduation ceremony held outside on the green.

Finally, the two professors who stand out in my UMBC memories are Ed Orser and Trudy Hamby. They were both gracious, brilliant, and inspirational. They each came into my university life at times when I needed that push or kind word to remind me of the potential I had within me.

I can't believe that it has been 50 years since my UMBC graduation, and I am astounded by the amazing transformations that have taken place there during these five decades. I do treasure some of my UMBC memories and the cherished friendships that have endured through all those years.

After UMBC:

- Received Master's Degree in Special Education from Loyola College in 1979
- Special education teacher in Baltimore City Elementary Schools for 19 years
- Purchasing agent at Bell Atlantic in Arlington, VA and Baltimore for 11 years

- Lived in Colorado Springs for 3 years and directed a before/after school program for a year.
- Worked as a cashier in a small casino in Cripple Creek CO
- Owned a small business in Eureka Springs, Arkansas for 4 years.
- Now happily retired living in Arbutus, MD.

UMBC University Singers

This Belongs to Robert Wobbeking '71, Economics

I Served on the Court

Being a man of few words my memories include being a Charter member of the Chess Club and Charter Member of the Tennis Club, for which I was #1 player all 4 years. I was also President of the Class '71 in my Junior year.

My friend Tom Berlin suggested a Chesapeake Bay Retriever as the UMBC Mascot in a contest AND won! The first Mascot was named "Sam".

After UMBC:

- Taught school for 31 years in Baltimore City.
- Football official since 1985.
- Track official since 1993.
- Ravens "Chain Gang" since 1996, sideline official for first-down measurements!

UMBC Tennis Team, 1970

This Belongs to William (Bill) P. Zaruba '73, History

Diggin' It

High school didn't really prepare me for college. It lacked preparations for study, test preparation, practical writing, and thinking skills. UMBC was a commuter campus when I began in the fall of 1969. The campus was small; it had the library, commuter cafeteria, gym, biology, math, and science buildings as well as the Hillcrest Administration Building. I liked Hillcrest because it was the only building on campus that gave the university an "Ivy-League" feel. And later, adding a Rathskeller.

It was difficult for me to adjust to the campus regime. I was struggling and after my first year, I was on academic probation. Once I found a course major in which I felt I could succeed (History), my life at UMBC began to flourish. It all began in the fall of 1971 with Dr. Storch's course, The Roman Empire. I discovered "Ancient Studies" and the fellowship of faculty and students became a lasting part of my life. I had classes with every Ancient Studies professor with the exception of Marilyn Goldberg and Carolyn Koehler. I became a member of the Classics Club and was its secretary for several years. I also participated in many events the department held in the fall celebrating Ancient Studies Week.

Also having an interest in Archeology, I enrolled in several of Dr. Karen Vitelli's classes. In the fall of 1972, I participated in the campus's archeological dig 18BA71 and the following spring participated in the publication of the site report. After graduating in 1973, I continued to participate in many Ancient Studies events. In 1981, I enrolled in my first Ancient Studies trip to England and Greece. And in 1984, again to Greece. During this trip, I met a young lady, Connie Flizanes, (Chemistry 1984) who several years later would become my wife. I continued to study Classics and in 2005, earned a second undergraduate degree in Ancient Studies with a focus on Ancient Greek. And how ironic it was that my wife is Greek as well.

During the mini-semester of 1986, I participated in my third Ancient Studies travel-study trip to England and the Netherlands where we toured at The Hague's Peace Palace. Amsterdam was just as intriguing with its famous canals and Anne Frank House.

I kept in touch with the department and faculty over the years, in particular with Dr. Jay Freyman who has seen our family grow over the years to the present day. Both my wife and I have fond memories of bringing our boys to campus to visit with Dr. Freyman when he was Dean of the Honors College.

In the Spring of 1973, I also attended a retreat at the University of Maryland's Donaldson Brown Center. There was a toga party there but no orgy - just an informal lecture and movie, neither of which I can remember. On Saturday morning, a modified Olympic Games comprising of a sack race and a foot race was held. Both Dr. Vitelli and Dr. Sherwin participated in the races.

One Ancient Studies class I remember was taught by Dorothy Kent Hill, the former curator of Antiquities at the Walters Art Gallery. Dr. Hill passed before the end of the term. It was a very somber time. I was asked by the department faculty if I could write an obituary for Dr. Hill and the memorial was printed in the Res Classicae, the Ancient Studies Newsletter.

I have such fond and pleasant memories of my time at UMBC. It was a period in my life in which I felt like I flourished due to the intimacy that was offered by the faculty members. After my trip in 1981, the participants were invited to Dr. Sherwin's home, where we met his family members. Both Connie and I attended a few of the pot-luck dinners hosted during Ancient Studies Week and Connie also had an opportunity to meet faculty and other diners. On one occasion, the dinner was catered by Ikaros Restaurant and faculty member Dr. Vitelli led the group in Greek dancing.

It has been fascinating to see the campus grow from a small, rural commuter school with a handful of buildings to the extensive and internationally-known campus it is today. I am so proud to be an alumnus of UMBC and also of its accomplishments achieved under the leadership of Dr. Freeman Hrabowski.

After UMBC:

- Worked as a Check Processing Specialist for the Federal Reserve: Baltimore Branch from 1979 to 2008.
- Attended UMBC part time and earned a 2nd B.A. Degree in Ancient Studies in 2005.
- Met Connie Flizanes, a UMBC grad (1984-Chemistry) on an Ancient Studies trip to Greece.
- Married in 1988 and are blessed with 2 sons, Michael and Nicodemus.
- My wife and I now reside in Ridgely, on Maryland's Eastern Shore.

Card Players in the Cafeteria

Dr. Freeman A. Hrabowski, III

UMBC President, 1992-2022

When I heard about the idea for this book, a compilation of stories from alumni of UMBC's first four classes, I couldn't help becoming excited about capturing the amazing spirit of these founders and pioneers. As Diane Tichnell writes, it was an exciting time, with the sense of something "fresh and new," both on the campus and in the country. The stories that she and her classmates share in these pages evoke a range of emotions. I laughed reading about Ed Doyle's efforts to melt the cheese on the vending machine cheeseburger he purchased at the cafeteria. I nodded in recognition thinking about the experiences of young people coming to a deeper understanding of themselves and their place in the world during a time of rapid and wide-ranging change.

At the time of UMBC's founding, the Higher Education Act of 1965 had just become law, and only 10 percent of Americans had graduated from college. That law both reflected and reinforced a shift in sentiment about access and opportunity, and more American families than ever were thinking about the possibility that their child could go to college. UMBC was one of the beacons of hope that emerged during that period. At a time when other universities had been around for a century or more, here was a new campus full of possibilities.

Realizing those possibilities required creativity, optimism, and often courage. Donna Helm writes about arriving on campus at a newly constructed parking lot from which she could see the university's three buildings set in a "sea of mud crisscrossed with plywood sidewalks." She went on to study French and to make lifelong friends. Dale Gough, just out of high school, came to campus to see about a job on the grounds crew. He arrived to find Dr. Albin Kuhn, UMBC's founding chancellor, out in a tractor mowing what grass there was. He took the job, and also decided to study at UMBC, basing his decision in part on the example of a university leader who was willing to step in and do whatever job needed doing. Other alumni write of their experiences playing on UMBC's early sports teams, participating in social protests, or performing in campus theatrical productions.

In some cases, the stories highlight the many ways life has changed. That job on the grounds crew paid just $1.35 an hour. Microwave ovens were still a relatively new technology. And the university's phone system required the attention and expertise of a switchboard operator who served both as a welcoming voice greeting callers and as a source of support and guidance for the many work-study students who learned from her.

While much has changed on our campus and in our society, the central themes of these stories still hold true. UMBC has always been a community based on strong relationships and a shared sense of what we can achieve together. It is a rare institution that has global reach and also has founders who can reflect on those early days while still finding creative ways to build on that vision. These stories chronicle the development and history of UMBC, and they also document the culture of America. They also reveal the many ways that events of that period shaped UMBC as the socially engaged university that it is, with a strong focus on solving real-world problems.

Dr. Valerie Sheares Ashby

UMBC President, 2022

As I have been so warmly welcomed into the UMBC community, I have enjoyed learning about the university's beginnings from our very first graduates — the group we affectionately know as "The Founding Four." What a treasure it is to have this collection of memories for future generations to learn where we began and for us to build upon the vision we share. UMBC may have started as three buildings and a sea of mud, but the tremendous progress made over the last 56 years and this enduring community tells me that we have only bright years ahead.

Tags: These are just some of the topics found in the memories:

Faculty/Favorites/Inspirational
Courses/Favorites
Firsts
Commuting
Friends
Theater
Dr. Kuhn
Social Unrest
Unforgettable Characters
Cafeteria
Early/First Days
Student Workers
The Library
Music
Vietnam/The War
The Concert
Diversity
Speakers/Guest Performances
Staff
New Buildings
Social Life
Choosing UMBC
Hurricane Agnes
Women's Issues
Mentorship
Dorms Open
Student Activities

Children brought to class
Parking
Protests
Campus growth
"The Red Brick"
Labs
Good Preparation
Falling in Love
Hillcrest
Veterans
Earth Day
Men's Sports
Women's Sports
Study Abroad
First Graduation
Creating a Party School
Foreign Language Study
Race Relations/Racism
Growing Up
Postgame Celebrations
Registering for Class
Sports
The Draft
Segregation
MiniMester
Student Organizations
Activism

Acknowledgements

This Belongs to Us was made possible by many members of the UMBC community.

Your editors, Diane, Dale, Mimi and Bob are very grateful to:

Founding Four Alumni writers who shared their stories

UMBC President Dr. Freeman Hrabowski who believed in us

Greg Simmons '04 MPP, Vice President, Institutional Advancement

Lisa Akchin, Associate Vice President, Engagement, and Chief Marketing Officer

Stanyell Odom, Director, Alumni Engagement

Jess Wyatt, Associate Director, Alumni Engagement

Kim Robinson, Senior Development Officer, Institutional Advancement

Colin McFarland '22, Technical Assistant

The UMBC Archives in the Special Collections, Albin O. Kuhn Library

Jim Lord '99, Director of UMBC Creative Services

The Founding Four Committee:

Royce Bradshaw '70	Joan Costello '73
Linda Crites '72	Bob and Mimi Dietrich '70
Ed and Sharyn Doyle '70	Mary Wyn Gillece Dudderar '70
Sandy Geest '72	Dale Gough '70
Donna Helm '70	Donna Banks Hekler '70
David R. Herron' 71	Betty Huesman '70
Louise Goodrich Izat '70	Fran Allen Nickolas '70
Carl Sallese '70	Marty and Jackie Schlesinger '71
Diane Juknelis Tichnell '70	Bill Wade '72

If these memories from the Founding Four Alumni at

the University of Maryland Baltimore County

inspire you to support UMBC, please consider making a donation to

one of the selected funds of your choice at the UMBC Foundation, Inc

at *umbc.edu/giving/founding four book*

All contributions are administered by the UMBC Foundation Inc. for the benefit of UMBC

Made in the USA
Middletown, DE
31 May 2023

31797922R00115